A PRIMER FOR DAILY LIFE

STUDIES IN CULTURE AND
COMMUNICATION
General Editor: John Fiske

A PRIMER
FOR DAILY LIFE

Susan Willis

London and New York

First published 1991
by Routledge
11 New Fetter Lane, London EC4P 4EE

Simultaneously published in the USA and Canada
by Routledge
a division of Routledge, Chapman and Hall, Inc.
29 West 35th Street, New York, NY 10001

Typeset in 10/12pt Linotron Baskerville by
Rowland Phototypesetting Ltd, Bury St Edmunds, Suffolk
Printed and bound in Great Britain by
T. J. Press (Padstow) Ltd, Padstow, Cornwall

British Library Cataloguing in Publication Data
Willis, Susan
A primer for daily life. – (Studies in culture and
communication).
1. Popular culture
I. Title   II. Series
306.1

Library of Congress Cataloging in Publication Data
Willis, Susan.
A primer for daily life / Susan Willis.
p.   cm. – (Studies in culture and communication)
Includes bibliographical references and index.
1. Consumption (Economics) – United States.
2. Capitalism – United States.   3. Suburban life –
United States.   4. Culture.   5. Social values.
I. Title.   II. Series.
HC110.c6w55   1991
307.74'0973 – dc20   90–47383
ISBN 0 415 04180 5
ISBN 0 415 04181 3 pbk

CONTENTS

ACKNOWLEDGMENTS

To liberate daily life from abstraction, I rely on:

partners in spunk, to spark the critical imagination
companions in struggle, to affirm the goal of socialism
and sometimes,
                              sweet passion

The people who are these for me
I acknowledge on this page
and in ways more personal

AUTHOR'S NOTE

In calling this book *A Primer for Daily Life*, I want to recognize and at the same time separate these observations from the pioneering work done by Henri Lefebvre and Michel de Certeau towards the development of the concept of "everyday life" (*"la vie quotidienne"*) and its theoretical apprehension. "Everyday life" originates in a European response to the development of mass culture, and it is fundamentally rooted in urban experience. My aim is to preserve their focus on mundane social life and practice, but to situate this in a more properly US and suburban context.

The bottom line in daily life is the commodity form. Herein are subsumed all the contradictions of commodity capitalism and our aspirations for their utopian transformation.

1

UNWRAPPING USE VALUE

Everything is packaged. Late twentieth-century commodity production has generated a companion production of commodity packaging that is so much a part of the commodity form itself as to be one of the most unremarked features of daily life. Only when we have to drag all those 30 gallon black plastic trash bags out to the curb or haul them to the town dump are we likely to grasp the enormity of packaging. Otherwise, it goes unnoticed even in drug stores and discount department stores where fully 80 per cent of the merchandise is packaged. Whether items are individually boxed or mounted for display on strips of cardboard backing, most packaging today includes a plastic see-through window or bubble. Packaging catches the consumer's eye, even though as a phenomenon of daily life, it is all but invisible. The package is a device for hailing the consumer and cueing his or her attention, by the use of color and design, to a particular brand-name commodity. The plastic cover replicates the display case or store window and suggests that each and every item is worthy of display.

Packaging also enables the standardization of weights and measures. For today's consumer, the "net weight" label is the only guarantee that a box of laundry detergent indeed weighs 4 lb or that the peanut butter in a particular jar really does amount to 1 lb 2 oz. The standardization of weights and measures represents a rationalization of sales similar to the Taylorization of production. In the workplace, Taylorization increased efficiency and productivity because in breaking production down into rationalized units, it offered the owners of the means of production greater control over the production process and a more systematic exploitation of the workforce. Taylorization has its end in the consumption of rationalized commodity units. Many of the basic foodstuff items that fill our kitchen cupboards today, such as crackers, cereal, flour, and pickles, were originally sold in bulk. Richard Ohmann describes the moment when Quaker Oats were first available as a packaged commodity, and develops the relationship between early instances of mass commodity packaging in the late nineteenth century and the expansion of the professional class, the first class in this country to function *en masse* as consumers (Ohmann, 1988). By comparison with commodities previously sold in bulk, mass-produced and packaged commodities, like Quaker Oats in the original 2lb package, were advertised as a more efficient means to buy and store basic household necessities. While it is true that increased urbanization from the 1890s on meant that more and more families did not have storage space for bulk merchandise, the underlying effect of mass commodity packaging is to break sales down into standardized units, thus enabling commodity producers to have greater control over consumption and a more systematic means of exploiting the consumer through advertising. Prior to the 1890s, there was no advertising for what would later become Quaker Oats, because, if such advertising had existed, it could only have promoted oats in general. The point of advertising is the designation of the commodity (and, by extension, the consumer) as a discrete unit.

The immensely popular advertising campaign devised for marketing California raisins suggests a new conceptualization of the commodity in keeping with postmodern capitalism. Where raisins from California were once marketed according to specific brand-name identities such as "Sun Maid," they are now promoted as the "California Raisins" and embodied in a band of wrinkly faced black "dudes" with skinny arms and legs, who chant "I Heard it Through the Grapevine" while soaking up the California sun. "California Raisins" do not represent a return to the pre-brand-name generic commodity, but rather the hyper-commodity whose connection to rock music and black culture heroes precipitates a vast array of spin-off products, from grotesque dolls to beach towels emblazoned with the "Raisins." If brand-name marketing represents the Taylorization of consumers, mass-marketing spin-off advertising is the postmodern form. Rather than fragmenting the broad mass of consumers into discrete and manageable units, postmodern advertising assumes a consuming subject capable of being interpolated from a number of angles at once. We will consume the "California Raisins" even if we never eat dried fruit.

Another significant function of packaging is to promote the notion of product purity. When Henry P. Crowell first packaged oats, he marketed them as "pure" by comparison with oats sold in bins and exposed to the air as well as the hands and coughs of salespersons. In late twentieth-century consumer culture, hygiene has complex ideological associations, most of which derive from the notion of progress which makes a primary distinction between the developed societies of the First World and the underdeveloped societies of the Third World. Purity is synonymous with the modern First World supermarket, where items are discretely shelved; bruised fruit, greying meat, and milk past its freshness date are removed; and where everything is enveloped in air-conditioning – yet another form of packaging whose frigid, artificial air exudes the very notion of purity. After all, germs cannot survive freezing temperatures; and in the First World, purity means being germ-free, even if the elimination of microbes requires heavy doses of pesticides, chemical preservatives, fumigation, radiation, and other artificial stratagems. To the First World imagination, the open-air markets of the Third World are a riot of impurities. The aromas of ripe fruits, meats, and cheeses cannot be conceptualized without the consequent horror of bacteria. Foods brimming over in baskets or loosely arranged on counters, in bins, or on the pavement suggest an indiscrete mingling of merchandise – and worse yet, people. In the First World, the package is the fetishized sign of the desire for purity, which, in the fullest sense, is also a desire for security. The ultimate outrage in commodity capitalism is product adulteration. Haunting the desire for purity are the tales told of food-service workers who, when angry or bored, spit, even urinate, into the not yet frozen or sealed TV dinners. Similarly, the consumer's desire for security meets its most chilling nightmare in the case of the deranged product tamperer, for whom the security seal on a bottle of Tylenol is a challenge to cyanide.

These functions of packaging and their ideological implications demonstrate that the throwaways of commodity consumption may well offer the most fruitful way into the culture as a whole. While the foregoing themes may well be complex and interesting, none, however, really scrutinizes packaging as a dimension of the commodity form itself. Such an analysis would look at packaging as a metaphor for the formal economic contradiction of the commodity. In *Capital*, Marx initiated his analysis of the entire system of capitalist economic relationships with an account of the commodity form. This is the nexus of capitalism as well as the means of understanding contradiction. Where Marx began with the commodity, I would begin to understand the commodity as it is metaphorically reiterated in its packaging.

3

Of all the attributes of mass-produced commodity packaging today, the most important is the use of plastic. The plastic cover acts as a barrier between the consumer and the product, while at the same time it offers up a naked view of the commodity to the consumer's gaze. Sometimes the plastic covering is moulded to fit the contours of the commodity and acts like a transparent skin between the consumer's hand and the object. Shaped and naked, but veiled and withheld, the display of commodities is sexualized. Plastic packaging defines a game of câche – câche where sexual desire triggers both masculine and feminine fantasies. Strip-tease or veiled phallus – packaging conflates a want for a particular object with a sexualized form of desire.

Packaging prolongs the process of coming into possession of the commodity. A buyer selects a particular item, pays for it, but does not fully possess it until he or she pulls open its plastic case or cardboard box. Possession delivers a commodity's use value into the hands of the consumer. Packaging acts to separate the consumer from the realization of use value and heightens his or her anticipation of having and using a particular commodity. Packaging may stimulate associations with gift-wrapped Christmas and birthday presents. However, plastic commodity packaging reveals what gift-wrapping hides. The anticipation we associate with the gift-wrapped present is for the

unknown object. In anticipating a plastic-wrapped commodity, we
imagine the experience of its use since its identity is already revealed.
In all our experiences of consumption, we are little different from the
child who convinces his mother to buy the latest Ghostbuster action
figure. From the moment he picks the packaged toy off the shelf, to the
moment he passes through the checkout, he will trace the contours of
the package with his hands, attempt to scrutinize the toy's detail with
his eyes, and lose himself in imagining how it will finally feel to push
the lever that makes the Ghostbuster's hair stand on end and eyes pop
out with fright at the delightfully cold and gelatinous slime – also
included in the package, but not yet available to the touch.

Tania Modleski, in her analysis of soap operas (Modleski, 1982),
makes a point about the genre's form that provides a clue to the
deciphering of commodity packaging. Modleski identifies "waiting"
as the most salient formal feature of soap operas. As we all know,
nothing ever really happens nor is any problem ever fully resolved in a
soap. The characters who open a particular episode may drop out of
sight for a day or two, a character might announce a dramatic or
scandalous event, but its culmination and consequences may drag on
for weeks. Viewers learn to hold plots and people in suspension,
waiting from daily episode to daily episode in unbelieving anticipation of dénouement. As Modleski puts it: "soap operas are important
to their viewers in part because they never end . . . The narrative, by
placing ever more complex obstacles between desire and fulfillment,
makes anticipation an end in itself" (Modleski, 1982: 88). Modleski
astutely compares waiting as a formal feature of soap operas with the
lived experience of the housewife. Alone at home, her husband at
work, some or all of her children at school, the housewife performs all
the daily chores necessary to maintain house and family in an
all-encompassing ambience of waiting:

> Soap operas invest exquisite pleasure in the central condition of
> a woman's life: waiting – whether for her phone to ring, for the
> baby to take its nap, or for the family to be reunited shortly after
> the day's final soap opera has left its family still struggling
> against dissolution.
>
> (Modleski, 1982: 88)

Modleski concludes that the appeal of soap operas resides in the way
they make waiting enjoyable. The soap opera turns waiting into
an aesthetic. This, then, lifts the housewife viewer out of her real

and frustrating experience of waiting, and allows her to apprehend waiting as pleasure.

I would extend Modleski's observations to the way we as consumers relate to the use value of commodities. Mass commodity packaging makes the anticipation of use value into an aesthetic in the same way that the soap opera transforms waiting from an experience into a form. Moreover, commodity packaging defines the anticipation of use value as the commodity's most gratifying characteristic. No commodity ever lives up to its buyer's expectations or desires. This is because in commodity capitalism, use value cannot be fully realized, but rather haunts its fetishized manifestations in the objects we consume. This is true regardless of our economic level of consumption. The shoddy purchase that does not fulfill its advertised promise promotes the pleasurable anticipation of the next (hopefully less shoddy) purchase. Similarly, the high-class piece of merchandise, for instance the sumptuous and expensive new fashion, that in itself seems to live up to all our expectations, also activates anticipation for the next purchase when we take our designer fashion home and hang it next to our now worn and boring collection of clothes. In defining the anticipation of use value as the site of pleasure in the commodity form, capitalism puts the consumer (whether woman, man, child, or adult) in a position analogous to Modleski's housewife. Waiting can only be rendered aesthetically pleasing to someone who is socially isolated and powerless. The housewife who comes to appreciate waiting as pleasure hardly has access to another, more active and affirming mode of getting through the day. Similarly, the consumer learns to associate pleasure with the anticipation of use value simply because commodity culture does not offer use value itself as appreciable or accessible.

Commodity capitalism fully develops the anticipation of use value while use value itself seems to serve no other purpose but to create the basis for its anticipation. Such a separation between anticipation and use value underlies Wolfgang Haug's *Critique of Commodity Aesthetics*. Haug focuses on advertising in order to develop a definition of commodity fetishism in the context of late capitalism. He draws on Marx's definition of commodity fetishism, but translates the Marxian contradiction between exchange value and use value into the terms of the market economy where the primary contradiction is between buyer and seller. Where Marx saw the commodity form as the embodiment of human labor in the abstract and this as the basis for its creation of exchange value, Haug sees the commodity's use value pressed into the service of sales. The buyer "values the commodity as a means for survival," whereas the seller "sees such necessities as a means for valorization" (Haug, 1986: 15). Haug concludes that commodities have a "double reality." First, they have a use value; "second, and more importantly, the *appearance* of use value" (Haug, 1986: 16). For Haug, the appearance of use value is essentially "detached" (Haug, 1986: 17) from the object itself. This is the aspect of the commodity form that advertising seizes upon and renders sensually perceptible in its words and images. The aspect of the commodity form that Haug defines as appearance would seem to correspond with the category of anticipation. Both suggest that the fetishization of the commodity is for the consumer the fetishization of use. Marx recognized this when he commented: "whenever, by an exchange we equate as values our different products, by that very act, we also equate, as human labour, the different kinds of labour expended upon them. We are not aware of this, nevertheless we do it" (Tucker, 1978: 322). The abstraction of labor which is the real basis of the fetish quality of commodities, is not something we as consumers can directly grasp, rather it enters our daily life experience as the inability to apprehend fully or even imagine non-fetishized use values.

Haug's account of commodity aesthetics, particularly the way he sees human sensuality wholly inscribed in the appearance of use value, where it is abstracted and turned into market value, bears a strong resemblance to the way in which earlier Marxist intellectuals developed the notion of reification. The landmark text on reification is included in Georg Lukács' *History and Class Consciousness*. Lukács begins with Marx's notion that "in the commodity the social character of men's labour appears to them as an objective character stamped upon the product of that labour" (Lukács, 1971: 86), and develops the point that commodity fetishism is both an objective and a subjective phenomenon (Lukács, 1971: 87). Objectively, there is a world of commodities and a market economy, whose laws we might apprehend, but which nevertheless seems to obey "invisible forces that generate their own power" (Lukács, 1971: 87). Subjectively, people in commodity capitalism experience the estrangement of their activities as these, too, become commodities. Crucial to Lukács' definition of reification is the notion that once labor power comes into being as the abstraction of human activity, it extends its influence to human qualities and personality as well. Such objectification, coupled with the highly fragmented and rationalized process of capitalist production, produces "the atomization of the individual"

(Lukács, 1971:91) in consciousness as well as labor. Reification defines the translation of commodity fetishism into human experiential terms.

> The transformation of the commodity relation into a thing of "ghostly objectivity" cannot therefore content itself with the reduction of all objects for the gratification of human needs to commodities. It stamps its imprint upon the whole consciousness of man; his qualities and abilities are no longer an organic part of his personality, they are things which he can "own" or "dispose of" like the various objects of the external world. And there is no natural form in which human relations can be cast, no way in which man can bring his physical and psychic "qualities" into play without their being subjected increasingly to this reifying process.
>
> (Lukács, 1971: 100)

Common to both Lukács' and Haug's analyses of the commodity form is the notion that under capitalism human qualities and the sensual dimension of experience are objectified and abstracted – or "detached" – from people and their activities so that they become commodities in their own right, "reified" or "aestheticized." The problem is, then, how to reverse – or break through – the process so as to recover and affirm all the human qualities that the commodity form negates by abstraction. The most challenging thinking along these lines is Theodor Adorno's *Negative Dialectics*. Like Lukács, Adorno sees consciousness – our mode of conceptualizing self and world – inexorably shaped by capitalism. Adorno too draws directly on Marx's theory of the commodity, particularly the phenomenon of equivalence. In order for exchange to take place, commodities, which would otherwise be distinct because of their vastly different properties, must achieve equivalence. As previously remarked, it is the abstraction of labor into labor power that produces equivalence. As Marx put it, "the equalization of the most different kinds of labour can be the result only of an abstraction from their inequalities, or of reducing them to their common denominator, viz. the expenditure of human labour-power as human labour in the abstract" (Tucker, 1978: 322). Where Marx uses the term "equivalence," Adorno, whose argument is more properly philosophical, develops the notion of "identity" (Adorno, 1973: 146). The whole of *Negative Dialectics* is aimed at "breaking through the appearance of total identity," in order to smash the "coercion" (Adorno, 1973: 146) of identification as a form that has its roots in economics and dominates all human endeavor and thought.

> The [exchange] principle, the reduction of human labour to the abstract universal concept of average working hours, is fundamentally akin to the principle of identification. [Economic exchange] is the social model of the principle, and without the principle there would be no [exchange]; it is through [exchange] that nonidentical individuals and performances become commensurable and identical. The spread of the principle imposes on the whole world an obligation to become identical, to become total.
>
> (Adorno, 1973: 146)

Adorno sees the possibility of negative dialectics in the fact that capitalism as a system and as a form of consciousness is both total and not total. The abstraction of human labor that permits equivalence both denies and requires the existence of multiple and qualitatively different labors. This is capitalism's contradiction. According to Adorno, contradiction "indicates the untruth of identity" (Adorno, 1973: 5) – not because it affirms some wholly other position outside of capitalism, but because it is "nonidentity under the aspect of identity" (Adorno, 1973: 5). *Negative Dialectics* holds tremendous possibilities for rethinking and reclaiming daily-life social practice under capitalism, because unlike the concept of reification, it apprehends fetishism as a tension between the abstracting forces of domination and their utopian antitheses. But how are we to apprehend contradiction? Adorno equates the possibility of contradiction in capitalism as an economic system with the possibility of realizing contradiction in thought. As he sees it, the translation of things into their conceptions leaves something out: a "remainder" which functions as the concept's contradiction. The project of translating negative dialectics into daily life would, then, require ferreting out all the remainders – the resistant, and perhaps quirky, material of practice and relationships that cannot be assimilated in the process of coming to equivalence.

Negative Dialectics is written as an unrelenting exposé – of the overwhelming tendency toward identity and its manifestations in philosophical thought. In the more mundane world of daily life, negative dialectics opposes the homogenization of mass culture, where standardization is marketed as a sign of quality, and the great range of qualitatively different social and cultural forms is transformed into the design details of commodities. What is most interesting about Adorno's writing is that while the notion of identity and all its ramifications are wholly revealed, the category of "non-identity" is never fully described, or analyzed. Adorno implies that to do so would dissolve the contradictory character of "nonidentity." The closest Adorno comes to specifying "non identity" in philosophical terms occurs in his introductory remarks, when he states that "what defies subsumption under identity [is] the 'use value' in Marxist terminology" (Adorno, 1973: 11).

This brings the discussion back to the initial problem of whether or not use value can be recognized and appreciated in commodity capitalism – or if, as Haug and Lukács affirm, the consumer is by definition embraced by abstraction and knows use value only as an "appearance" or "reification."

Contrary to this line of reasoning, there is another wholly different approach to Marxist popular culture criticism that abandons the possibility of redeeming concrete use values, and turns instead to the area of appearance as the only social reality in capitalism and, therefore, the only possible site for the transformation of social life. In this approach, appearance comes to mean something more than it does for Haug, as it takes on the complex proportions of the imaginary. Where Haug defined the appearance of use value as a wholly fetishized and manipulated concept, the imaginary is seen as a highly conflictual zone that brings together social and psychic life, needs and desires, and where the forces that seek to dominate, control, and recuperate social life are contested by desire, meaning-making, and a full array of practices that connote cultural resistance. This definition of the function of the imaginary in popular culture originates in Walter Benjamin's landmark essay "The work of art in the age of mechanical reproduction." This may well be the single most important essay in the development of Marxist popular culture criticism. It assesses the influence of mechanical reproduction in a bold and liberatory way. Yet many students today fail to grasp the revolutionary thrust of the essay, and apprehend it instead as a nostalgic complaint for the loss of "aura," the concept Benjamin uses to describe all the unique magical qualities of great traditional art. How is it possible to construct two very different readings: the one revolutionary, the other nostalgic? It may well be that Benjamin intended his reader to have to deal with nostalgia. After all, we are all products of the class history that privatized art, privileged its meanings, and thus endowed it with "aura." Furthermore, we have not attained the socialist transformation of society that would allow us fully to understand the democratizing potential of mechanical reproduction. To this end, Benjamin uses phrases that inevitably elicit regret. He describes "aura" as "withering" (Benjamin, 1969: 221) and tells us that mechanical reproduction "depreciates" (Benjamin, 1969: 221) art. Even his use of "authenticity" (Benjamin, 1969: 220) to designate original works of art is apt to stir up a longing for something concrete – even if it is bought at the price of private ownership.

> The technique of reproduction detaches the reproduced object from the domain of tradition. By making many reproductions it substitutes a plurality of copies for a unique existence. And in permitting the reproduction to meet the beholder or listener in his own particular situation, it reactivates the object reproduced. These two processes lead to a tremendous *shattering* of tradition which is the obverse of the contemporary crisis [facism] and the renewal of mankind. Both processes are intimately connected with the contemporary mass movements. Their most powerful agent is the film. Its social significance, particularly in its most positive form, is inconceivable without its destructive, cathartic aspect, that is, the *liquidation* of the traditional value of the cultural heritage.
>
> (Benjamin, 1969: 221)

Here Benjamin defines two points that have become fundamental to much recent work in Marxian popular culture criticism: (1) mechanical reproduction destroys traditional forms and their meanings; and (2) in "meet[ing] the beholder or listener in his own particular situation," the reproduction enables people actively to make their own cultural meanings. The elimination of "aura" is thus the basis for a radically optimistic definition of mass culture. Contemporary interpreters of Benjamin include Dick Hebdige, whose work on British youth subcultural groups demonstrates how such groups "shatter" traditional definitions of race and class and use music and dress to make new social meanings (Hebdige, 1979). Another contemporary exponent of Benjamin is John Fiske, who develops countercultural readings of shopping malls and supermarkets based on the notion of making meanings. Fiske sees all activities that run counter to the demands of production and consumption ("hanging-out in shopping malls") as instances where we as individuals control and define use. Fiske's point is that supermarket foods may be fetishized commodities, but when we take them home and work them into a meal – be it ordinary or special – we make daily-life cultural meanings (Fiske,

1989). The critic who best sums up this approach to mass culture, and who explicitly links his work to that of Benjamin, is Simon Frith, whose book on rock music, *Sound Effects*, portrays culture as a struggle over meanings. Paraphrasing Benjamin, Frith points out that once "the artistic authority of cultural goods had been broken, their significance had become a matter of dispute: the ideological meaning of mass culture was decided in the process of consumption, and the grasping of particular works by particular audiences was a political rather than a psychological event" (Frith, 1981: 57).

Some problems arise when Benjamin's observations on the mechanical reproduction of art are brought forward into the present. Benjamin's essay responds to a moment in the history of cultural production when film was still fairly new and the notion of a non-reproducible art had not as yet been eclipsed by the wholesale mass production of culture. By comparison with our own moment in history when the desire for music is met by radio, record, tape, or CD, and drama can mean up to two or three rental videos a night, Benjamin, in his *Moscow Diary* (1986), recounts a world where the theater was a regular component of the day's activities and where shopping for a child's gift meant purchasing a handcrafted toy. Do we as a culture have any sense of what a non-reproducible audio or visual work of art might be? When Benjamin says that film has the power to smash traditional art forms and their inscribed meanings, he documents a world that better remembers traditional forms and their traditional meanings.

By comparison, late twentieth-century capitalist culture is cluttered with an ever-expanding array of already reproduced works of art. In such a world, the struggle over meanings often defines cultural commodities in conflicting ways. A 1988 TV advertisement for the Las Vegas narcotics squad portrayed the "narks" in the dress and language of the youth gangs who are "traditionally" cast as dopers and dealers. The "narks" were shown to have a battering-ram equipped vehicle whose special audio system blasts rap music, also traditionally associated with street gangs, while it batters down people's doors. Today, subcultural groups are indeed making meanings and smashing traditions, but so, too, are the forces of containment. Once meanings become detached from their inscription in traditionally defined class art, they, like the cultural objects themselves, can be used – defined and redefined in almost any way to serve almost any class interest. The critic engrossed in mass culture as a struggle over meanings runs the risk of being captured in a system of ricocheting – sometimes revolutionary and sometimes recuperated meanings. Such a view of society and such an approach to culture may not be in a position fully to grasp contradiction. While it articulates the liberatory potential of cultural practice, it may stop short with a reading of culture that cannot escape its own description of resistance and recuperation. This is because the concept of making and struggling over meanings is not primarily based on an understanding of the commodity form. It assumes the commodity as an unavoidable fact of mass culture, but does not question the consequences of fetishism on the meanings made.

The Marxian account of commodity fetishism does not represent a negation of use value. Rather, it demonstrates that use value is dialectically referred to in our fetishized objects of consumption, just as all of mass culture is haunted by the desire for non-alienated social relations. This mass culture cannot fulfill, even while its utopian possibility sustains daily life. The essays in this book are aimed at revealing some of the ways we do indeed recover use value in daily-life social practice, use value that largely goes unrecognized because, living in a world that tends toward homogenization, we are ill-equipped to think dialectically and have very few models that exemplify contradiction of the sort Adorno defines. Nevertheless, the entire system of capitalism is predicated on the production of use values, just as it is motivated by exchange value. In Adorno's terms, "the utopia [promised by the realization of use value] extends to the sworn enemies of its realization" (Adorno, 1973: 11). Use value exists in all of its negations. It is undeniable, even while it is denied realization. The great problem that occurs when we contemplate how use value might be made visible is that once we make it accessible to critical discourse we risk transforming it into another reified object for consumption. Adorno's reluctance to flesh out the category of non-identity may well stem from his recognition that to do so he would either risk "relinquishing the otherness in dialectics" (Adorno, 1973: 375) or he would end up positing something so transcendent as to become solid and "arrest dialectics" (Adorno, 1973: 375) entirely.

Nevertheless, contemporary mass culture yearns for the recovery of use value. Nowhere is such yearning more explicit than in the historical theme park. Some, like Mystic Seaport in Connecticut or Calico Ghost Town in California, are more commercially oriented than others, such as Sturbridge Village in Massachusetts. All occupy authentic historical sites that have been refurbished and opened to the public as private or state-run tourist attractions. Historical theme parks have aspects of the theater, the museum, and the amusement park without wholly replicating any of these. They put the late twentieth-century visitor into the re-created daily-life context of a 100-year-old town, a 200-year-old village, or a 300-year-old fort. Tourists wearing T-shirts and shorts, carrying cameras and pushing baby strollers, share a cobble-stone or packed-earth road with the park's costume-clad employee hosts, whose dress meticulously replicates all the social strata of the park's historical referent. In the historical theme park, "You are there," you are "in" history in a far more real and tangible way than was ever possible in the early 1960s TV dramatization that took this phrase for its title.

The visitor to a historical theme park is free to wander in and out of the site's various buildings with no more than a map or a schedule of events as a programmatic guide. Throughout the park – in its schoolhouse, forge, or ship's store – the material culture is rarely displayed as it would be in a museum; rather, it is performed. At Mystic Seaport, there are cooperers, smiths, caulkers – all of them plying their trades. While making their wares, the tradespeople explain the process and the use of their goods to the tourists. In this, the costumed role-players necessarily betray the authenticity of the historical experience as their pedogogical function requires them to explain rather than theatrically enact what might have been daily-life conversations.

The growing number and popularity of historical theme parks today testifies to a strong curiosity about and attraction to societies where the production and exchange of useful objects was the tangible basis for the way people defined themselves in community with others. In such a society, the objects of daily life were the bearers of a particular tradesman's care and craft. The same could be said of the implements and skills that defined women's domestic labor. The historical theme park allows the visitor fully to imagine what it might have been like to live in a culture where use values more directly shaped lives and relationships than they appear to do in late twentieth-century capitalism. This does not occur in a traditional museum, where the visitor might find all the same objects that exist in a particular historical theme park. Objects in a museum do not suggest use values even though they may readily be perceived as useful. Everything from Native American bone needles to colonial spinning wheels is defined, by the very nature of the museum, as an artifact: an object severed from its historical context, whose only current purpose is to be collected, studied, preserved, and displayed.

The artifact underscores the visitor's role as spectator rather than participant; someone wholly isolated from the social and historical context that produced the object and able to apprehend it only as a curiosity.

I would argue that this is not the case when, during the process of putting in a garden or rummaging through an abandoned shed, we turn up a horseshoe or some other piece of long disused farm machinery. The discovery of a historical object during the course of our own daily-life activities, defines us as something more than spectators. We might be tempted to compare our world and the sort of activities we perform with the imagined world of the object when it was in use. The question is whether such musing inevitably slides into nostalgia. Many of us will find Adorno's flat declaration that "The right to nostalgia cannot be validated" (Adorno, 1982: 109) much easier to affirm than it is to achieve. Nevertheless, those instances when we actively come upon the past are better able to produce critical rupture with the present than is possible when the past is merely displayed for us. The horseshoe that we turn up, that abrupts into the normalcy of digging in a garden, is very different from a horseshoe mounted on a wall and perceived as a decorative object. While every encounter with the past runs the risk of recuperation, those moments when we use the past to engage with the present have the power to escape nostalgia.

A trip to a historical theme park is never a wholly nostalgic experience. This is because the visitor is not only a spectator, but a participant in communication with the role-players and in the recreation of the world of the past. The historical theme park may be likened to a stage play where the audience joins the actors on the stage. Indeed, this is how Walt Disney first defined the relationship between the visitors to Disneyland and the costumed role-playing employees who do everything to maintain his "magic kingdom," from sweeping the streets to selling the tickets and parading about disguised as Mickey or Pluto. The extensive portfolio handed out to employees at the original Disneyland in California dispenses with the notion of work and employees by renaming all jobs according to the language of theater and film. Most workers are designated as players; managerial people are stage managers and set directors. The recent opening of the Disney–MGM Studios Theme Park in Florida climaxes the transformation of labor into a commodity by incorporating the visitor consumer more fully into the spectacle of production. Here, the visitors are costumed and made up in order to join the paid employee role-players in the recreation of TV dramas such as *I Love Lucy*. The Disney people call it "interactive entertainment." What is interesting is the way this theme park problematizes the function and relationship of actor and audience; and with it, worker (producer) and consumer. But the impulse to think through these relationships creatively is foreclosed by the way the amusement park is not conceived as a site of production, but is felt instead to be a commodity itself. The labor of the paid employees and the unpaid labor of the consumers is wholly devoted to producing and maintaining the park as a simulacrum of Hollywood in the 1940s, complete with palm trees, the Brown Derby Restaurant, and Chinese Theater.

What sets the historical theme park apart from Disneyland, even if the former includes rides on bygone buggies, boats, or railroads, is that the production of amusement is secondary to the production of the historical setting. In the historical theme park, work is a performance whose theatricality is obscured by the totality of the world being created. The only historical discrepancy is that the objects produced in the historical theme park will never be sold or used as they were originally intended. The candles may be hand-dipped to historical specification, but they will be sold in the park's gift shop as Christmas presents for people who light their homes by other means.

Even if the image of historical totality disintegrates at the point of sales and use, the performance of work in historical theme parks may at times appear to transcend theatricality. A friend, Alexander Wilson, when researching a book on the construction of landscape in capitalism, told of a visit to Old Fort William in Thunder Bay, Canada. It was mid-December; a light snow was falling. Besides himself there was only one other visitor to the park. Nevertheless, there were some twenty costumed employees busily tarring canoes, repairing traps – doing all the things that the original residents of the fort did during the winter months to ensure production during the spring, summer, and fall. With only two paying visitors and twenty paid employees, the distinction between amusement park, theater, and the real production of eighteenth-century daily life is significantly blurred. In order for the historical theme park successfully to create history as "aura" – that is, embued with time and place, as Benjamin defined it – it has to produce its use values all year round. A historical theme park that only functioned seasonally would not escape theatricality and amusement.

We need not go so far as Thunder Bay, or even Sturbridge Village, to witness the fully theatrical production of use value. Today's neighborhood supermarket is in many respects a mundane version of the historical theme park. Indeed, the supermarket is something of a postmodern museum of the third world, whose displays of exotic fruits and vegetables, such as breadfruit, cactus apples, passion fruit, star fruit, and horn melons often include museum-like inscriptions, such as this one from a San Diego supermarket: 'Cherimoya, prized by the Incas, now grown in Santa Barbara." Where the supermarket most closely replicates the historical theme park is in its presentation of labor. The current practice in many supermarkets is to put a theatrical form of production on display, while the real work that goes into maintaining the store and serving the customers is either hidden from view or made to appear trival because of deskilling. The work of pricing the merchandise, stocking the shelves, cleaning the store, and preparing the meat and produce for sale is accomplished by a largely invisible workforce, whose members labor behind the scene in a backroom warehouse, or at night after the store is closed. The work of managing, which includes decisions over purchases and personnel, is conducted by a number of upper-level employees whose photos sometimes decorate the store's service counter, but who are seldom seen by shoppers. The work of checking, which in a bygone era would have anchored the customer's apprehension of work in the supermarket, has today been greatly undermined by the installation of computerized scanners that weigh and price the commodities and often speak to the customer. The supermarket checker has been deskilled to the point of becoming a human robotoid extension of the checkout system.

As if to compensate for the marginalization and in some cases the erasure, of productive labor, the supermarket offers an array of theatrical labors, whose importance has more to do with the spectacle they create than the actual services they render. Most supermarkets today offer in-store bakeries, deli-counters, florist shops, and gourmet food sections. These are staffed by a corps of store personnel whose uniforms are more theatrical than practical. Often, the employees' pert hats and aprons mimic the colors and patterns of the store's interior decor, making the supermarket something of a stage for sales and the costumed employees the actors enacting service. If we take the supermarket as the place where we most commonly come into contact with the fetishized commodities of daily life, then all the strategies developed by the supermarket to render service personnel, to make it visible, redound in a theatricality whose effect is to create the appearance of use value in the commodities we buy. This is most clearly the case when one of the costumed employees stands mid-aisle, blocking shopping cart traffic, and commences to operate one of the store's speciality machines. These include coffee grinders, orange and grapefruit juicers, peanut-butter mills, and pineapple corers. The employee who husks and cores pineapples to produce those Dole-like rings does so with a single thrust of a chrome-plated lever. The performance brings the image of work and a wholesome product into the shopping area.

This is an instance where labor is truly rendered as performance; and hence, a commodity – customers consume the spectacle of work whether or not they actually buy the pineapples. Such spectacle stands in the place of any reference to the hundreds of laborers who cultivated, harvested, packed, shipped, and marketed the pineapple. Their erasure from the commodity form is the basis of its fetishism. The impossibility of retrieving their labor in the supermarket setting condemns the attempt to create use values to spectacle.

There is one perspective on use value that I have not as yet brought into this discussion. It is by far the most radical, the most utopian, and the most difficult to imagine how it might be translated into daily-life social practice. I am referring to Jean Baudrillard's critique of political economy, and with it Marxian theory, which he sees as replicating the mode and logic of capitalism. According to Baudrillard, the construction of value under capitalism, which derives from the relationship of exchange value to use value, is homologous to the system of signification defined by Saussure, where meaning is born of the relationship of signifier to signified. This defines a more fundamental unity between consciousness and capitalism than obtains in Lukács' theory of reification. For Baudrillard, the logic of capitalism is the logic of meaning.

In such a system, there is no possibility of a redemptive notion of use value. Rather, it (like the concrete and the referent) is implicit in the structure of capitalist economics. For Baudrillard, use value cannot in any way oppose exchange value, undermine it, or offer an alternative to it; rather, use value ensures exchange value and underwrites its centrality. Hence, according to Baudrillard, any critique of consumer society that posits use value as its point of critical distantiation or its transcendent "other" (as my own efforts aim to do) is inevitably inscribed in the logic of capitalism. As Baudrillard flatly puts it, use value does not exist, except, perhaps, as capitalism's "alibi" (Baudrillard, 1988: 71).

In fact the use value of labor power does not exist any more than the use value of products or the autonomy of signified and referent. The same fiction reigns in the three orders of production, consumption, and signification. Exchange value is what makes the use value of products appear as its anthropological horizon. The exchange value of labor power is what makes its use value, the concrete origin and end of the act of labor, appear as its "generic" alibi. This is the logic of signifiers which produces the "evidence" of the "reality" of the signified and the referent. In every way, exchange value makes concrete production, concrete consumption, and concrete signification appear only in distorted, abstract forms. But it foments the concrete as its ideological ectoplasm, its phantasm of origin and transcendence ["*dépassement*"]. In this sense need, use value, and the referent "do not exist." They are only concepts produced and projected into a generic dimension by the development of the very system of exchange value.

(Baudrillard, 1975: 30)

Baudrillard challenges us to think outside of value altogether. How might we begin to imagine a society devoted to the elimination of value? Baudrillard appeals to the work of the anthropologist, Marcel Mauss, whose elaboration of the gift ("*le don*") in primitive society offers an alternative to societies based, like our own, on accumulation rather than dispersal. Central to Mauss' description and to Baudrillard's analysis is the annual potlatch ceremony practiced by the Kwakiutl Indians where accumulated wealth and possessions were not just redistributed, but wholly used up. Baudrillard sees the potlatch as the basis for reciprocal social relations, based on a form of exchange that destroys value. Baudrillard's term for such a social dynamic is "symbolic exchange," which he alludes to as the anti-form of capitalism, whose cursory and subtle manifestations might be glimpsed at unexpected moments even in consumer society. Baudrillard cites play, the spontaneous gift, destruction as pure loss, and symbolic reciprocity as examples of symbolic acts (Baudrillard, 1988: 93). As social forms, these are hardly fully realized in our daily lives. Many readers come away from Baudrillard's illusive descriptions of the symbolic dissatisfied at not finding more fully fleshed out images of alternative practices. Indeed, all of Baudrillard's examples of symbolic exchange present themselves as somewhat inaccessible to discursive elaboration. As Baudrillard allows us to imagine it, the symbolic might erupt out of the economic fabric of capitalism as it does when workers initiate a wildcat strike; or it might trick us, like a *trompe-l'œil*, seduce us unawares, causing received cultural meanings to disintegrate. The oblique references to the symbolic that emerge in Baudrillard's writing bear a striking resemblance to the way Adorno presents the negative dialectic. We can not imagine what the negative dialectic would really look like as a social reality, nor can we grasp what our daily lives might be like if we fully participated in symbolic exchange. This is because capitalism is a totality. Both the negative dialectic and symbolic exchange are "elsewheres" (Baudrillard, 1988: 71) that cannot possibly be fully realized or apprehended in capitalism. Then, too, any attempt to render the symbolic concrete risks reification and the cancellation of its alterity.

What is clear is that today's so-called aberrant forms of consumption, which we might be tempted to interpret as negations of value, are, instead, affirmations of value. For instance, imagine a society whose dominant social form is anorexia. Would a society that absolutely denies all forms of consumption abolish value? According to Baudrillard's account of use value as the alibi of exchange value, the renunciation of consumption in a highly commodified society such as our own merely affirms the fact of consumption, as well as the power of temptation and revulsion associated with commodities. Unlike the potlatch, an anoretic society would not destroy accumulated value, rather it stands as firm testament to the dead weight of value. Unlike the community of Kwakiutl, whose social relationships are the expression of reciprocity, a society of anoretics exemplifies the extreme isolation of the individual, whose only, and overwhelmingly obsessive, relationship is to the rejected world of commodities.

What about a bulimic society? Would a society that consumes "to the max" finally use everything up and therefore eliminate value? By comparison to Baudrillard's definition of the potlatch where a community's wealth is used up in order to prevent accumulation, the cycle of bulimic engorgement, evacuation, engorgement merely demonstrates that the supply of commodities is never-ending and cannot ever be used up. In consumer society, bulimia is the antithesis and the negation of potlatch. Where potlatch disperses desire and enables gratification, bulimia is burdened by desire and the impossibility of ever attaining satisfaction. Bulimia does not destroy value, rather it flattens the distinction between exchange value and use value, by rendering all value equal to consumption.

As social forms, anorexia and bulimia are not "other" to capitalism. They may be labelled "consumption disorders" but they express the formal logic of capitalism. A radical theory of use value would resist the desire to render it concrete, and therefore readily imaginable and easily instituted. A facile notion of use value as a whole term conditions the impulse to imagine that either a bulimic or an anoretic society represents an anti-capitalist definition of use. Gayatri Spivak warns against similarly simplistic conceptualizations of use value when she states that students who claim they "read literature for pleasure rather than interpretation" or academics who take pride in their hands-on word processor production techniques are merely fulfilling romantic notions about use value as having something to do with handicrafts and barter (Spivak, 1987: 162). Spivak argues for a "discontinuous" theory (Spivak, 1987) of use value in keeping with Adorno's notion of the negative dialectics, and I would say Baudrillard's sense of symbolic exchange. Spivak sees use value as a "classic example of a deconstructive lever" (Spivak, 1987: 162). This means that it has the potential to undermine and transform the logic of capitalism, because, according to Spivak, it "is both outside and inside the system of value-determination. It is outside because it cannot be measured by the labor theory of value" (Spivak, 1987: 162) and because we can conceive of things being use values without their being accessible to economic exchange. However, use value is inside the system of value because there would be no possibility of exchange value without it. This makes use value an unstable category. It is never whole, or concrete. In it, "there is something left untranslated (not included in the system of value determination), which is its contradiction". This is what Spivak means when she defines use value as "discontinuous" and therefore capable of putting "the entire textual chain of value into question" (Spivak, 1987: 162).

I challenge the reader to resist reading prescriptive models of use value into the following essays.

BACKGROUND SOURCES AND
FURTHER READING

The dialectics of use value

In *Capital*, volume I, parts I and II, Karl Marx defines the commodity form, commodity fetishism, use value, exchange value, labor power, and the creation of surplus value. These concepts are essential to all considerations of value in capitalist society. Other examples of dialectical criticism that bear on the question of value include the following.

Adorno, Theodor (1973) *Negative Dialectics*, London: Routledge and Kegan Paul.

Baudrillard, Jean (1975) *The Mirror of Production*, St Louis: Telos Press.

——(1981) *For A Critique of the Political Economy of the Sign*, St Louis: Telos Press.

Goux, Jean-Joseph (1990) *Symbolic Economies: After Marx and Freud*, Ithaca: Cornell University Press.

Spivak, Gayatri (1987) *In Other Worlds*, London: Methuen.

Commodity fetishism

Studies in advertising lead the way in defining commodity fetishism in late twentieth-century capitalism.

Haug, Wolfgang (1986) *Critique of Commodity Aesthetics*, Minneapolis: University of Minnesota Press.

Leiss, William, Kline, Stephen, and Jhally, Sut (1988) *Social Communication in Advertising*, London: Routledge, Chapman and Hall.

——(1985) "Magic in the marketplace: an empirical test for commodity fetishism," *Canadian Journal of Political and Social Theory* 9 (3).

Marchand, Roland (1985) *Advertising the American Dream*, Berkeley: University of California Press.

Williamson, Judith (1978) *Decoding Advertisements*, London: Marion Boyars.

2

GENDER AS COMMODITY

"Are there girls and boys?"
"No, just boys and boys."

In late twentieth-century capitalism, gendering has invariably to do with commodity consumption. We buy into a gender in the same way we buy into a style. It makes no difference whether we choose unisex or an ultra-feminine image, the act of buying is affirmed and the definition of gender as commodity is maintained. As Marx defined it, the commodity form is the negation of process and the social relations of production. When gender is assimilated to the commodity, it is conceived as something fixed and frozen: a number of sexually defined attributes that denote either masculinity or femininity on the super-market shelf of gender possibilities.

Currently, we witness the wholesale, uncritical acceptance of the word "gender" into professional discussions and practice. To give an example, I recently attended a women's faculty committee meeting where the discussion focused on salary discrepancies between men and women employees. The word "gender" was the single most frequently used term and it never designated anything more than men versus women. In fact, the discussion of the university's use of gender-based studies of salary seemed to suggest that the only gendered subjects are women. Such widespread uncritical usage of the term relegates gender to a one-dimensional conceptualization of men and women. It negates the possibility of seeing gender socially and historically, and it promotes the essentialization of sex as the basis for gender definition.

To free gender from the commodity form requires seeing it as an ongoing expression of how we live our sexuality, something that emerges out of social relationships and in relation to larger social forces. Such a conceptualization of gender would be analogous to

23

conceiving and creating objects in terms of use value alone. The challenge gender poses to feminists is to confront the structure of capitalism in our daily lives. To strive for gender as process as opposed to gender as commodity is to seek a basis for human variety and wholeness in a society where commodification equates wholeness with surfeit and variety with perversion.

To understand how the commodity form is integral to gender, we must first realize the influence of commodities on the process of gendering. Our culture is mass culture, where one of the strongest early influences on gender is the mass toy market. It is strikingly appalling that in today's toy market there is a much greater sexual division of toys defined by very particular gender traits than has ever existed before. The recuperation of sex roles in the eighties is a stunning reversal of the Women's Movement in the late sixties and early seventies, which called into question children's sex-role modeling. Dress codes were condemned, co-ed sports flourished, fairy tales were rewritten, and toys were liberated. We tend to imagine that our parents and grandparents conformed to strict sex-role modeling practices. And we like to think that the cultural turmoil of the sixties changed everything. The fact is, in mass culture today there is an ever more rigidly defined separation of the sexes based on narrow notions of masculinity and femininity. Walk into any toy store and you will see, recapitulated in the store's aisle arrangement, the strict distinction and separation of the sexes along specific gender lines: Barbies, My Little Ponies, and She-Ras in one aisle; He-Man, the Transformers, and ThunderCats in another. It little matters that many nursery schools now mix the dolls and trucks on their play-area shelves if everyone – children in particular – perceives toys as originating in a boy-versus-girl context. Commodity fetishism erases production and presents the toy store (or TV commercial) as the toy's point of origin. Children have difficulty conceiving of their toys as having been made. Many who do not yet read often refuse to believe that the writing on a doll's back spells out "Mattel," rather than the doll's name. In denying their toy's connection with corporate production, children fully live the fantasmagoric relationship to objects that Marx identified as synonymous with the commodity form. For the young child, toys have no reality previous to their display on the toy-store shelf, where each conforms, as if by magic, to a clearly gendered universe.

Children do not question the toy store's boy-versus-girl universe, nor do they conceive of such a universe having been produced. This is

Photo: Karen Klugman

because the labor of stocking the shelves is largely performed after hours. The young child's apprehension of gender is really no different from the way we as consumers tend to see commodities as autonomous. The consummate realization of commodity fetishism, which derives from the erasure of production, is the child's view of banks. Most young children see the bank as a window that dispenses cash to people whenever they run out of it. Parents who try to explain the realities of cheques and savings deposits quickly realize how difficult it is to restore notions of production in a consumer-oriented society. In the toy store, the essentialized notion of gender (and the boy-versus-girl universe) fall apart only when the mass-produced toy falls out of favor. Reduced for quick sale, it is thrown helter skelter into a "sale" basket with other out of favor toys where gender, like the toy itself, no longer matters.

To highlight the retrenchment of gender in the eighties, I want to cite two people whose experience of the child's relationship to gendering and commodities is closer than my own. The first is my daughter, whose comment, made almost a decade ago when she was three, gives simple and direct testimony to the young child's recognition of polymorphous, or multidimensional sexuality. When asked whether her teddy bear was a boy or a girl, she responded, "My teddy is both a

25

boy and a girl." Later, when I came to write on Toni Morrison and wanted to characterize the author's portrayal of childhood sexuality, I remembered my daughter's remark and referenced her in my essay (Willis, 1987b). Many readers have told me that what they most remember about that essay is Cassie's comment. Such response registers acceptance of the way professional women and their children can work together in critical pursuits. But I would say that the deepest appreciation is for Cassie's fresh affirmation of multiple sexuality and the refusal to be made into one or the other.

I want to compare Cassie's comment to a response made just the other day by my 4-year-old son. Cade was playing with some foam-rubber dinosaurs, whose lack of sexual characteristics makes them comparable to the teddy bear. I asked him whether his dinosaurs were girls and boys. "No," he said, "just boys and boys." In its syntax, his remark suggests the possibility of masculine and feminine, even as his words affirm that boys can only be boys and play with boys. Clearly, little boys in our society are more strongly determined in their conception of sex-role differences than little girls. Parents seldom reprimand little girls for dressing-up in boys' or men's clothing. But all the day-care teachers I have spoken with report that most parents show some degree of displeasure (occasionally rebuke and violence) for their young sons who experiment with skirts and gowns while playing dress-up. Notwithstanding social pressure, I think the real difference between my two children's remarks has more to do with history. Cassie's comment reflects the mid-seventies, while Cade's speaks for the mid-eighties and the absolute retrenchment of gender based on essentialized notions of sex.

Before going on, I want to emphasize that listening to what children say can contribute to a critical perspective and a professional practice. It is extremely important for intellectuals and academics to heed a community of voices including racial minorities, the elderly, and children. Some of the best creative writers have opened their ears and consciousness to childhood experience. Often, the fiction that articulates the adult writer's perception of society through the eyes of a child is most astute in its comprehension of social contradiction. Faulkner's great short stories, such as "Barn Burning," Paule Marshall's *Brown Girl, Brownstones*, and Toni Morrison's *The Bluest Eye* all grasp the critical significance of the child's perspective. Children recognize the contradictions adults take for granted because they are not yet fully inscribed in capitalism either as the producers or reproducers of the system. Not too many generations ago, children were brought into

26

capitalist production as workers when they were 10 or 11 years old. Today the situation is different. Now capitalism seeks to incorporate children as the reproducers of society. Children learn and want to be consumers at an ever earlier age. Ten or fifteen years ago, children did not shop regularly for toys nor did they make specific demands for toys much before five years of age. Today, 2- and 3-year-olds request toys regularly. They know exactly what they want and the brand names as well.

Two of today's most popular children's toys are Barbie and He-Man. Barbie has withstood the decades with the same pert nose, frozen smile, pointy breasts, hard body, and pencil-like long and thin legs. In contrast, He-Man has had trouble remaining popular through two marketing years. His position as top boy toy was supplanted by Lion-O of the ThunderCat TV series and GI Joe, who returned from the Viet Nam era to rival the upstart Rambo. He-Man's precarious fame is symptomatic of the rapid turnover in the mass toy market. He-Man last year, Lion-O this year, next year some new "already legendary" folk hero without a past or a future. What is important in these TV series spin-off toys is that they all derive from the same basic model. Each has a different costume and a different range of super-powers, but all are young men with muscles and a mythic group of helpers who battle an equally muscled and mythic army of evil-doers. My reference to He-Man is thus a reference to this particular model of toy whose specific appearance depends on which legendary folk hero is currently being promoted in TV programming. Barbie and He-Man are both most popular with a particular age group of consumers. From my observations, I would say that 4- and 5-year-old boys want He-Man, whereas, girls from 5 to 7 want Barbie. (These ages are confirmed by the appearance of the children in the TV commercials for these toys.) No longer toddlers and not yet beginning to experience puberty, this age group in our society represents true childhood. Clearly, Barbie and He-Man do not offer the child the possibility of prolonging polymorphous sexuality or developing an open notion about gendering. Instead, they define the rigid separation of the sexes; and what is more, a narrowed conceptualization of gender. I want to expand on the latter. My hypothesis is that both toys play on the child's conscious and unconscious notions about adolescence. They focus the child's conception of the transformations associated with adolescence in a singular fashion, and they suggest that change is somehow bound up in commodity consumption.

Advanced capitalist society offers the child growing up very few means of registering the experience of individual development and bodily change except by way of commodity consumption. In the United States ritual ceremonies, such as the Jewish bar mitzvah or Catholic communion, that mark stages of growth and integration with the adult world, are marginalized, diminished, or assimilated to the commodity form. While the First World tends to perceive the rites of passage celebrated in primitive societies as backward or barbaric, these do satisfy the individual's need to focus the fears, excitement, and expectations associated with moments of change and to overcome these through group social practice. We may lack rites of passage, but we have not transcended the need to experience ourselves and our changes in relation to larger social groups of continuity. For most people growing up in the First World state, the birthday is the moment when the individual intersects with the desire for social gratification. We tend to experience our birthdays as absent rituals. This is especially true of children. They plan and discuss and imagine their birthday parties months in advance. Most often they talk about who will be invited to their parties, not as an exclusionary, but an inclusionary practice. In naming their guests, children conceptualize the social group that will observe their moment of transformation. Because it is important that the social group represent continuity,

Photo: Karen Klugman

children tell each other who will come to their parties all year round. Adults may think children are self-centered for wanting to imagine their birthday parties and name their guests at any time of the year. In doing so, they fail to realize that this is one of the ways in which children assemble an imaginary utopian social space.

Children live their birthdays as magical moments of change even if they are not celebrated with a party. Many children undergo emotion-fraught weeks leading up to their birthdays. When my daughter Stacy became 5, she demonstrated all the behaviors generally ascribed to women turning 40: sleeplessness, depression, touchiness, mood swings. For children, birthdays are more than abstract temporal moments that mark transition from one age to the next. They are felt to include actual physical transformation. I have heard more than my own children ask to be measured upon awakening on their birthdays, fully expecting to have grown an inch in the night. This demonstrates the child's awesome conceptualization of the body in time, and the powerful way in which the birthday focuses the desire for change.

Adolescence is the period when growth really does mean change. Young children anticipate adolescence both consciously and unconsciously. Desire, dread, fear, longing, curiosity, timidity, boastfulness are all bound up in the anticipation. It is interesting that in consumer society the child's anticipations are met more quickly and easily by commodities than by social institutions such as family and schools. Commodities offer young children a means to articulate their notions about the transition to adolescence. No matter what the adult (probably male) toy manufacturers had in mind when they created her, Barbie is for the 6-year-old girl the acquisition of the adult female body. Her accentuated length suggests height, which is the young child's most basic way of conceptualizing age or adulthood. And her accentuated breasts signify – directly and simply – femininity. Clearly, 6-year-old girls sense that adulthood and femininity are far more complex. If only through their parents, they experience the labor, care, worries, discussions, desires, and satisfactions that constitute adulthood. If only through their mothers, they know the shapes, softness, rhythms, odors, and expressions that define femininity. Barbie negates all of these, just as He-Man reduces adult masculinity to the simple formula of hard, overly muscled body.

Popular culture includes a long tradition of male superheroes, such as Superman, Captain America, and Batman, whose physical strength and super-powers imply the penis and give expression to the power and domination associated with the phallus. He-Man is a part of this tradition. But for the young boy of 4 or 5, muscles mean muscles. He-Man's muscles bulge so grotesquely that my own son first called them "bumps." This is the commodity's one-dimensional definition of masculinity. It seizes one of the characteristics children associate with adolescence, a visible and controllable aspect (boys can work out with weights and control the size of their muscles), and makes this one trait take the place of the complexities it negates. Another toy currently marketed for young boys is a voice-transforming machine. The boy speaks into it and his childlike voice comes out dramatically deepened, although slightly roboticized. Like developing muscles for the first time, voice change can be a traumatic experience for the adolescent boy. The voice-transforming machine teaches young boys that commodities have an easy answer for what would otherwise be a difficult, perhaps painful, situation. The familial relationships that might help a child through awkward periods of development are put aside, supplanted by a magical machine.

In analyzing the relationship between adolescence and commodities, I am focusing on a single moment in the child's relationship with the toy. This is the moment when desire is enacted in consumption. It does not matter whether the child actually buys the toy or merely

Photo: Karen Klugman

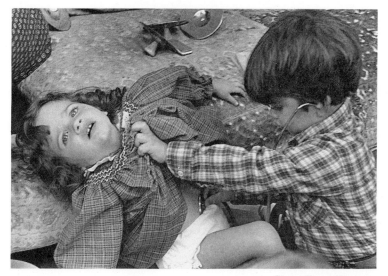

Photo: Karen Klugman

voices desire: "I want that!" In advanced consumer society, the act of consumption need not involve economic exchange. We consume with our eyes, taking in commodities every time we push a grocery cart up and down the aisles in a supermarket, or watch TV, or drive down a logo-studded highway. The visual consumption of the commodity form is so much a part of our daily landscape that we do not consciously remark how meanings are inscribed in such acts of consumption. Banana-sticker logos offer a case in point (see chapter 3). We need not buy bananas in order to have consumed the notion of the corporate state which is abstracted, miniaturized, and emblazoned on each and every banana skin.

What the child does with a commodity is another situation entirely. The analysis of children's play with Barbie and He-Man alone would fill a book. Barbie can slide down avalanches just as He-Man can become the inhabitant of a two-storey Victorian doll's house. I have observed such situations and day-care teachers can describe thousands more where play disrupts gender roles. Ivan Illich suggests an interesting way to understand the function of play when he characterizes women's domestic labor as the work of putting "utility" into the hollow commodities that fill up daily life (Illich, 1982). As he describes it, women's "shadow work" transforms the meaningless store-bought egg into an ingredient for a meal, which then constitutes social relationships and wholeness. Leaving aside the nostalgic tendency to resurrect peasant society that is present in Illich's writing, I would say that children's play functions along these lines. Children transform commodities into use values and use these as a means for articulating their social relationships. What is more, they do not recreate lost values or bygone forms of utility, as Illich would have the contemporary housewife somehow dredge up the long lost relationship of the peasant woman to the freshly laid egg. Rather, children's play produces newly imagined social possibilities, where gender is no longer the most essential attribute, but one quality among many other interesting human features.

I want to look at the moment of consumption more closely to demonstrate that no matter how deeply it articulates our inscription in capitalism, it also includes utopian dimensions, particularly for children. Buying is a form of exchange where the social interaction that defined older systems such as barter is reduced to the universal equivalent: money. In buying Barbie or He-Man, the young child is able to experience the transition to adolescence as an act of consumption. However, because young children do not control money, nor have they been taught to think abstractly (this is the point of the first-grade arithmetic lesson that uses nickels, dimes, and quarters as counters for addition and subtraction), the child's experience of consumption is somewhat different from that of the adult. Even if the child performs the purchase with money he or she received as a gift or an allowance, the moment of exchange includes dimensions of play-acting, mimicking what adults do when they hand dollar bills to the clerk and get change back.

For children, the moment of consumption, which for adults is focused primarily on pocketbook and cash register, is instead expanded to embrace the child's peer group of playmates. When a young girl buys Barbie or receives Barbie as a Christmas or birthday present, she experiences consumption in relation to a collectivity of young girls who have or want Barbies. The same group social practice that informs children's thoughts about their birthdays also conditions their acts of consumption. By comparison, most adults do not experience consumption as a form of reciprocal social practice. Competition, "Keeping up with the Joneses," is the fully deformed and commodified adult version of the child's sense of collectivity in consumption. Often adults mistake their young children's desires to have the same toys that other children have as a manifestation of greed or rivalry. A young boy who already has He-Man, Lion-O, and an assortment of their respective helpmates may well ask for GI Joe or

Rambo, not because he wants a more militaristic toy, but because a friend brought his GI Joe or Rambo to school for "show-and-tell." While such a child is indeed being conditioned by capitalism to consume, and consume massively, the child is simultaneously voicing the desire to participate in his friend's world and experience. Similarly, many children enjoy "sleeping over" at a friend's house, and young children often look forward to and discuss their first "sleepovers." This is how children break down the nuclear family and restructure themselves in a collectivity of caring. By playing with the friend's toys, eating at his or her table, watching the TV, and sleeping in the friend's bedroom and bed, the child makes the notion of the extended family a concrete experience. Just as children's play transforms commodities into use values, so too does their relationship to consumption reveal utopian social dimensions.

These examples of the social dimensions that haunt commodity consumption are all impoverished and contained by the larger system of capitalism. If young children recognize these social dimensions and bring them forth in their speech and play, while adults are blind and inured to them, it is because the child's experience of capitalism is less immediate – they are neither producers nor, for the most part, reproducers – and because their experience is simply less long. My intent is not to essentialize childhood, making it the equivalent of some basic human nature or state, but rather to show how the child's perspective is precisely historical and social. Because children come into the world dependent upon adults and older siblings for their care, their experience is primarily the experience of social interaction and relationships. Socialization into capitalism is a process of learning to substitute alienation and commodities for human relationships. When children recognize utopian social dimensions in otherwise highly commodified situations, they challenge us all to liberate the social from the commodity form. This is a revolutionary challenge. It is analogous to the challenge Marx made to the working class in the nineteenth century, to recognize and seize the buried human relationships in labor and in the products of labor which have been abstracted and alienated by wage labor and the commodity form.

Under capitalism our group social practice is commodity consumption. If we subscribe to the notion of gendering as process, and I think this is the only fruitful way to see it, then we must confront the fact that gender, like all our attributes and expressions, is bound up with the commodity form. The problem posed is how to define gender – and every other quality that marks the individual's intersection with society – in truly human terms. As I see it, there are two possible responses. The first, the separatist solution, holds forth limited success. In a society defined by sexism and male domination, lesbian separatism functions at the level of sexuality in a fashion similar to a homesteading community with respect to capitalist production and commodity consumption. Both represent a political choice, but neither is transformative of society as a whole. The problem with the separatist solution is its marginality. Either it is so different from dominant culture as to have no impact on the rest of society, or it includes points of attraction for capitalism, in which case it is readily co-opted and assimilated. The most to be gained from separatism is reform. Lesbian separatism can stimulate tolerance of alternative sexuality, but it cannot transform male domination in society at large. Similarly, communities based on alternative modes of production can promote an awareness of less exploitative economies and non-polluting energy sources, but these communities are not transformative of either capitalist economics or its relationship to petrochemicals, nuclear arms, and computer chips.

The most radical response to daily life under capitalism is to develop a mode of criticism and practice similar to that which I have been working towards here. This is a difficult task, because, lacking separation and autonomy, the cultural critic who addresses society from this point of view risks being engulfed or simply dismayed by the contradictions he or she seeks to reveal. The goal is to recognize in all our commodified practices and situations the fragmented and buried manifestations of utopian social relationships. The critique of capitalist culture extends from the culture industry into the most trivialized instances of daily life. This is a terrain of struggle where the desire to liberate social relationships runs head on into the forces of capital logic that stymie or bankrupt the imagination. Often movements that begin in opposition to capitalism fail to *trans*form the system and instead merely *re*form its structures. Witness the current debates amongst university faculties over the issue of maternity versus parenting leave as a case in point. Even if faculty members struggle for the more radical notion of parenting leave, their conceptualization of parenting and how such a leave would function is often assimilated to capitalist modes of thought. When the argument for parenting leave fails to treat men and women equally and instead posits a primary and a secondary caregiver, then what began as a radical and transformative goal merely recapitulates inequalities in the workplace which valorize one worker's eight hours over another's. If parenting cannot be promoted as a reciprocal endeavor, what chance is there of transforming wage labor itself? If we argue for change but maintain the structures of thought generated by capitalism, our actions fall short of producing transformation. So too with gender. The struggle to liberate gender does not aim to provide more genders, more commodified forms to choose from, but to enable people to experience gendering through human interaction and social practice.

There are really two threads to the discussion I have been elaborating here. One has to do with the individual's experience and desire, and the other with the larger notion of society itself. I want to make an analogy between the two. On one level children want to experience their individual changes concretely and socially; on another level I would say society as a whole longs to experience change and to register change as historically meaningful. We have seen how the young child's notion of change has largely to do with growing up and becoming an adult; and how change then is focused on adolescence and articulated in relation to gender and sexuality. What, then, might be the broader historical and social equivalents of the sort of changes individuals experience in their lifetimes? This is a difficult question because the same erasure of production that defines our experience as consumers, influences our relationship to history. We may well ask whether change under capitalism can even be conceptualized. Other societies have felt change, but do we? From our vantage-point in the late twentieth century, peasant society is perceived as boring and monotonous; yet this was a society deeply imbued by cyclical time. The meshing of production with the seasons meant that all life partook of the year's four climatic changes. In industrial society we no longer live with the seasons, but against them, working to maintain the same level of productivity, the same types of activities, no matter what the date or season. In writing the great critique of the eighteenth-century Enlightenment, Max Horkheimer and Theodor Adorno condemned the notion of progress. They saw it as the ideological means of exacerbating the class division of society, of enabling the greater technological exploitation of the workforce, and of the wholesale devaluation of the individual (Horkheimer and Adorno, 1972: xiv–xv). For Adorno and the other Marxist intellectuals of the Frankfurt School, time and history under capitalism are portrayed as an abhorrent and bleak sameness that recapitulates domination. Homogeneous time, this is how Walter Benjamin characterized capitalism's negation of change. It is a history propelled by the notion of progress, but going nowhere (Benjamin, 1969: 260–1).

Instead of change, capitalism is punctuated by events, such as moon shots and scientific discoveries; or by the horror of events, such as the nuclear holocaust. Of course, there are struggles for change: Civil Rights, the Women's Movement, anti-nuke and anti-war. But in a history dominated by progress these struggles can yield no more than reform.

Everything transforms but nothing changes. This is a fitting motto for late twentieth-century capitalism, particularly as it is embodied in the mass toy market. One hundred years from now, when anthropologists from another planet visit the earth and begin poking around in the heaped-up residues of our culture, they will find buried in the stratum marked "1980s" a vast array of toys whose singular purpose is to transform. Trucks, planes, boats, tanks, cars, helicopters, space vehicles, and submarines all turn into robots. Some robots turn into lions, insects, or dinosaurs. These are the Transformers, Gobots, and Dinobots. Often the complicated series of manipulations required to produce the transformation from car to robot and back again to car baffles the adult left reading the toy's instructions while the 4-year-old child, using fingers and intuition, performs the transformation unaided. What is interesting about the Transformers is the way the notion of transformation suggests spontaneity and change, while the reality of the toy teaches program and pre-programmed outcome. As children's fingers fold in axles and wheels and pull out arms and legs, they learn that change is already inscribed in the machine. The Popple offers another good example. This is an ugly sort of teddy bear in blotched pastels with a commodious pouch sewn into its back. By turning the animal head over heels and stuffing it into its own pouch, the child turns the Popple into a ball. This requires a fair amount of pushing and punching. In the end, change is defined as necessary, but abusive, with the strong arm of the child administering the Popple's transformations. Such toys weld transformation to consumption. They offer a notion of change in which program and domination prevail. These supplant the possibility of conceptualizing change in any other way. They are compensatory objects for individuals who cannot grasp history as personally meaningful.

The fascination with transforming toys may well reside in the utopian yearning for change which the toys themselves, then, manage and control. Much of popular culture, including animation as a form, expresses the same contradictory relationship between the desire for change and its control. As if by magic, animation makes lines move and brings figures to life. The illusion has nothing to do with magic but is, instead, produced out of a highly rationalized workforce and a deeply technologized production process. The intimate relationship between the desire for change and its control is memorably depicted by Mickey Mouse in the movie *Fantasia* (Willis, 1987a). As the Sorcerer's Apprentice, Mickey Mouse wiggles his magic fingers and brings a broom to life. This is a metaphor for the magic of animation. However, the single broom multiplies and becomes a threatening hoard of marching brooms. Only the intervention of the master, the Sorcerer, can restore order. His magical eyes ablaze, the Sorcerer embodies another metaphor; this time for the need to control the production process. Nowhere in our society are the contradictions of capitalist production rendered so visible – yet presented as if they were so "normal" – as they are in such examples from mass culture.

The icons of twentieth-century mass culture are all deeply infused with the desire for change. By comparison, the nineteenth century is populated by concrete, whole, growing – but never metamorphosing – folk heroes such as Paul Bunyan, Pecos Bill, and John Henry. These spoke for historical development and continuity and the centered, very solid construction of masculinity. This is certainly no longer the case with the advent of the twentieth-century superheroes. Superman, Batman, the Incredible Hulk, Spiderman, Aquaman, and all the other "-men" (as well as a few feminine adjuncts such as Wonder Woman), are locked on the perpetual articulation of the moment of transformation. Clark Kent/Superman, Bruce Wayne/Batman, Peter Parker/Spiderman, and now Prince Adam/He-Man – all the superheroes demonstrate that the conceptualization of transformation requires masculinity to be constructed as a duality. The weak, sometimes bumbling, even nurturing aspects of masculinity are portrayed as somehow necessary to the emergence of the superhero so long as these can be kept separate from the superhero's omnipotent form. Even Rambo, who appears to be integral, conforms to the dual notion of masculinity once his inferior Third World adversaries are taken collectively as his necessary, but antithetical, alter ego.

Peter Parker provides a clue to the interpretation of all the superheroes as representations of change on the individual level. He is perpetually caught at the moment of transformation from adolescence to adult manhood. No matter how many transformations he undergoes, Peter Parker never advances beyond high school and the chemistry test or basketball practice he inevitably misses in order to swing through the city as Spiderman. Similarly, Superman constantly regresses into Clark Kent's boyish ineptitude. Prince Adam/He-Man is the 1980s' version of the same superhero complex. Boyish in his humor, loving of parents, friends, and his giant pet cat, Prince Adam sports about the Palace of Eternia with very few duties, obligations, or woes. He-Man is in every respect Prince Adam's antithesis. Resourceful, courageous, dynamic, he battles the enemies of Eternia and bears the burden of his world's future. As in the case of his superhero predecessors, almost no one knows that mild-mannered Prince Adam is really He-Man. Hence, the transformation to He-Man is depicted and experienced as a moment of explosive and private power. Prince Adam seizes his sword, commands the power of Castle Gray Skull, and KABOOOOM!: "He-Man." Contrarywise, the transformation back to Prince Adam is portrayed as a moment of humiliation. Because he is never around during his people's crucial battles, Prince Adam is thought to be a "wimp," even by his father, King Randor, whom he most wants to impress with his super-powers. This traps Prince Adam in perpetual Oedipal anxiety. In chapter 4 I describe a female character who is similarly beset by Oedipal entrapment. Failure to resolve Oedipal desire for transcendence is one way in which these commodities define the consumer as dependent and disempowered.

It would be simplistic and reductive to interpret the Prince Adam/

Photo: Karen Klugman

He-Man complex as an extended metaphor for the penis, even though the sword, the sudden empowerment, and the return to relaxed wimpishness make the vulgar Freudian reading unavoidable. Similarly, it would be limiting and essentializing of the vulgar reading to interpret the dual construction of masculinity as two separate, perhaps age-differentiated but nevertheless equal, male gender possibilities. Such an analysis equates gender with a set of attributes and fails to recognize the historical implications of duality itself even as it fails to consider how gender and our thoughts about gender are bound up with our conceptualization of change. A critical approach guided by the notion of gendering would finally transcend the question of gender as a specific problem and recognize that gender is one of the ways in which we define relationships, identity, and change. The question from this perspective is not which is a better manifestation of gender, but how the construction of gender, particularly with respect to transformation and duality, begs the imagination of some alternative construction. If Prince Adam's transformation to He-Man and back again binds masculinity to a traumatic and unresolved notion of adolescence; and if this transformation functions in a larger sense as a figure for a society incapable of imagining real change, can we begin to imagine an alternative superhero – one who would not be integral and solid like the nineteenth-century Paul Bunyan, but who would totalize masculinity in another way by bringing all the dimensions of boyishness into his role as an adult man. When little boys buy Prince Adam to complement their He-Man dolls, they are affirming the separate and dual construction of masculinity, but they are also demonstrating an appreciation of all the boyish and nurturing traits Prince Adam embodies even as they yearn for He-Man's muscles. Uncovering the utopian aspects of the young boy's fascination with Prince Adam begs another, and with it a more radical, consideration: what about young girls? And what about girls and boys together? In a society dominated by mass culture and the commodity form, as ours is, is it possible to imagine a gendering process that boys and girls might experience reciprocally; or are there only Barbies and He-Men (or worse yet: "boys and boys")?

BACKGROUND SOURCES AND FURTHER READING

Another approach to gender is to consider its relationship to the politics of sexuality and sexual preference. The following texts look at forms of heterosexual marginality, lesbianism, and male homosexuality as these are conditioned by capitalist society and inflected by race.

D'Emilio, John (1984) *Sexual Politics, Sexual Communities*, Chicago: University of Chicago Press.

Rich, Adrienne (1976) *Of Woman Born*, New York: W. W. Norton.

Rubin, Gayle (1975) "The traffic in women: notes on the political economy of sex," in Reyna R. Reiter (ed.) *Toward an Anthropology of Women*, New York: Monthly Review Press.

——(1984) "Thinking sex: notes for a radical theory of the politics of sexuality," in Carole Vance (ed.) *Pleasure and Danger: Explorations in Female Sexuality*, New York: Routledge and Kegan Paul.

Smith, Barbara (1983) *Home Girls*, New York: Kitchen Table, Women of Color Press.

Zimmerman, Bonnie (1985) "What has never been: an overview of lesbian feminist criticism," in Gayle Greene and Coppelia Khan (eds) *Making a Difference*, London: Methuen.

3

LEARNING FROM THE BANANA

I want to suggest a method for looking at the phenomena of daily life that draws on the historical methodology defined by Walter Benjamin in his *Arcades Project* (Benjamin, 1989). While *Das Passagen-Werk* was published posthumously, I think the collection reveals enough about Benjamin's concept of history as it relates to the present and as it is articulated culturally to use this work as one possible way to begin to develop analyses of contemporary culture. What struck Benjamin in his consideration of the nineteenth-century Paris arcades was the dynamic juxtaposition these produced between the public and the private, with the shops carved out and constructed within older living space, and the way in which the shops referenced past historical periods and foreign geographies in their commodities and decor. From the juxtapositions Benjamin developed a materialist approach to history which he described as analogous to the theory of montage. He realized that the references to the past functioned as quotations; that is, the present embodies significant meaningful moments of the past and quotes these in its creation of the now. As defined by Benjamin, neither montage nor quotation suggests stasis as they now do in relation to structuralist and post-structuralist theory. Rather, they contribute to a dialectical reading of history – history defined not as a continuum projected out of the past and propelled by progress into the future, but history apprehended from our vantage-point in the present as ruptured moments that take on significance because of their relationship to the present. As he put it:

> Historicism contents itself with establishing a causal connection between various moments in history. But no fact that is a cause is for that very reason historical. It became historical post-humously, as it were, through events that may be separated

41

from it by thousands of years. A historian who takes this as his point of departure stops telling the sequence of events like the beads of a rosary. Instead, he grasps the constellation which his own era has formed with a definite earlier one.

(Benjamin, 1969: 263)

Contrary to the excitement Benjamin apprehended in the montage created by the Arcades, we in late twentieth-century society are apt to feel ourselves smothered or numbed by an apparently homogeneous cultural space. Shopping malls and supermarkets are hewn out of previously undeveloped tracts or built upon the destruction of urban neighborhoods. Either case precludes the possibility of producing the disruptive juxtaposition between past and present. Our dilemma is how to reverse the blind rush of progress and turn ourselves around, like Benjamin's description of the "Angelus Novus," moving backwards into the future with eyes "fixedly contemplating" the past. Our problem is how to recognize moments of rupture in a cultural fabric that appears all too continuous. The following essay/montage represents an attempt to read culture by looking backwards into history. Hence, our present cultural moment, defined here by the supermarket, tells us something about a text produced in a previous historical context. The essay quotes the earlier text in such a way that elements in the text are revealed that may not have been seen as primary when it was first produced. These elements, in turn, dialectically reveal more to us about our own historical moment. Literary purists may be horrified to find that I will read Faulkner through the optic of the supermarket. Similarly, cultural purists, who like to keep the media separate from other forms of popular culture, will be equally upset to discover that the consideration of banana-sticker logos renders visible the development of Mickey Mouse as an icon. What I am aiming at is the excitement and dialectical revelations that Benjamin captured in the *Arcades Project*. These may not be available to us except by making use of disruptive cultural juxtapositions whose relationships are *not* finally gratuitous, but instead define a "constellation" which our own "era has formed with a definite earlier one."

THE BANANA YESTERDAY: SUBSTITUTE SATISFACTION

In 1929 William Faulkner wrote *As I Lay Dying*; with it, he demonstrated how Georg Lukács' definition of typicality in the historical novel might be brought to bear on history's seemingly most insignificant characters, and how literary modernism might be conceived as the proper mode for the articulation of history. Lukács stressed the importance of conceptualizing history in relation to the social movements of "popular" forces. He advocated the use of "a 'middling,' merely correct and never heroic 'hero'" in order to demonstrate historical typicality. With reference to Walter Scott, Lukács states that "[he] lets his important figures grow out of the being of the age, he never explains the age from the position of its great representatives, as do the Romantic hero-worshippers' (Lukács, 1962: 39). In its depiction of a backward sharecropping family, Faulkner's novel translates "middling" into the social terms of American history. The novel tells of the death of Addie Bundren (the mother) and her family's hapless ten-day-long journey from their Mississippi farm to Jefferson where she will be buried. Hauled through flood, fire, and hot summer sun, the mother in her coffin is the novel's central figure, whose embrace widens to include her immediate family members, piled into a mule-drawn buckboard and accompanying her to her grave. These, history's forgotten characters, their concerns and the events that stymie their progress, can neither be trivialized nor dismissed. Rather, they have a strange power to reach across the decades. They fascinate and trouble our thinking. This is because Faulkner's portrayal realizes how people and populations that are economically marginal may well be central to history and to a particular epoch's mode of change.

Reading the family's journey from countryside to provincial metropolis as a historical metaphor allows us to see the plight of a single family as a figure for the migration of the country's agricultural workforce to the cities. The family's migration is a geographic metaphor describing demographic change. It also suggests the historical transition from a still large agricultural economy to something else – and here I hesitate over the term "industrial society." Although industrialization is part of the picture, Faulkner is describing a population who, as sharecroppers, can at best be considered marginally as producers; and who, when brought into industrialized society, will participate only partially. This is a population whose oppression was ensured by debt peonage and inefficient farming techniques. Sharecropping may have been the basis for the landowner's profits, but it did not provide large-scale accumulation either for the sharecroppers as a class or for the South in general. Rather, it solved the problems of excess labor at a time when there was no need for a larger urban workforce. It also ensured a labor reserve whose destiny was never full integration with industrial production except during periods of war (notably the Second World War, when thousands of tenant farmers left Appalachia and the Deep South for jobs in such cities as Muncie, Detroit, and Chicago).

Aside from the fact that much of Faulkner's writing, including his two long novels, *Absalom! Absalom!* and *The Sound and the Fury*, are concerned with telling the history of the South and, more fundamentally, with examining history in terms of social and economic factors, there are specific textual justifications for reading *As I Lay Dying* as a historical novel. The novel concludes with the long-awaited burial of Addie Bundren who, after ten days of Mississippi sunshine, has decomposed into a mass of fetid smells and burbling sounds. Burial signifies closure. It marks the fact that the mother has finally passed out of the family unit; and, in relation to the metaphoric interpretation I am developing, it marks the end of the world with which the mother is intimately bound up. Indeed, both the mother and her world are, in the novel's final page, replaced. "Meet Mrs Bundren" – with these, the novel's concluding words, the father introduces his new wife to his children only hours after laying their mother to rest. The father's unexpected and hurried marriage suggests at one level a crass attitude toward women, and at a more fundamental level it demonstrates the novel's dramatic leap into a world defined by a very different set of economic and social relations. This is because Anse's two wives represent the novel's two economic modes. Depicted both in life and in death as something primal, Addie is thought to be a fish at one point and later is described as an insect. Otherwise, Addie is often portrayed by the flux and flow of bodily fluids: the mother, producing fertile and nurturing liquids, and the corpse gurgling and simmering in its corruption. Often more earth than mother, Addie represents the unmediated connection with organic process. This is Faulkner's backhanded and disparaging mode of portraying what in another writer might well have taken on positive dimensions: that is, the fundamental and reciprocal relationship with the land which typifies agricultural communities. The long journey into town, more than the actual moment of Addie's death (which, in the novel, is ambiguous) or her final interment, describes the process by which the family sheds its connection with the land and with it relinquishes the agricultural mode of production.

The new Mrs Bundren, conveniently married at the graveside and ready to take her place in the family, represents a new set of connections and a very different economics. But before defining these,

I think it important that we realize just how cataclysmic is historical change in Faulkner's writing. We are here dealing with a novel where change is integrally bound up with the loss of certain individuals; either by death, or, in the case of another of the family's members, brutal incarceration. Darl, Addie's second son, is handcuffed and hauled off to an insane asylum at the close of the novel. The question we must ask is not whether Darl is insane, but what he represents in the novel. We might begin to answer this question by seeing Darl as a reiteration of his mother and her function. Indeed, Darl is described as most like his mother; so we might assume that he too represents a connection with the land and must, like his mother, pass out of existence with the transition from agrarian to urban culture. Darl's relationship with the land, however, is very different from the organic connection established with it by his mother. Throughout the text, whenever we as readers are placed inside Darl's narration, seeing the world through his eyes, we see a landscape transformed into a modernist painting. Distance is foreshortened and shapes otherwise held separate by a more perspectival point of view collide and become superposed. The mother's coffin resting on a pair of saw-horses is for Darl a "cubistic bug," while his perception of a horse, driver, and wagon merges to the point at which the horse appears to be wearing the driver's hat. Darl's way of seeing defines him more as artist than sharecropper, more visionary than aberrant. His arrest and incarceration brutally demonstrate that his alternative way of seeing has no place in the world defined at the conclusion of Faulkner's novel.

Just what is this new world I have been alluding to, then, whose rural roots have passed away and whose artists are incarcerated? I would suggest that Faulkner has captured a view of the world that we in the 1990s will grasp as our reality. To understand how *As I Lay Dying*, written on the eve of the 1930s, addresses conditions in the 1990s, we must return to the novel's concluding page, where we find one of the most dramatic images of consummate historical transformation ever depicted in fiction. Seated in the buckboard and munching bananas, the children are amazed to discover their father sporting a new set of false teeth and escorting the new Mrs Bundren. Her dumpy frame is made all the more cumbersome by the packaged graphophone she carries. With the bananas, teeth, and graphophone, the family has acquired three highly significant commodities to replace its lost members. With these three objects as well, the novel is catapulted out of its agrarian economic mode, where exchange has been based upon barter, and redefined squarely in consumer society.

In the largest sense, the insight that frames Faulkner's conclusion is the understanding that populations that cannot be brought into capitalism as producers are assimilated at the level of consumption. This was true during the 1930s when many people out of work or marginally employed still managed to save dimes, nickels, and soap coupons towards the purchase of "fiestaware," sheet music, and curios. And it is true today when commodities flood the ghettos and suburban shopping malls, transforming unemployed youths into full-time mall crawlers and consumption addicts for whom seeing is nine-tenths of possessing. Then, in a more narrow sense, Faulkner's conclusion demonstrates how commodities fill the holes in social relationships produced by the loss of mother and brother. If the commodity is by definition a fetishized object, containing the hidden social relationships of its producers, we have only to extrapolate from its production to its use to understand how the commodity conveniently fills the gaps in broken and alienated social relationships. Under twentieth-century capitalism, consumption becomes a means of replacing relationships between people and deflecting emotional responses which might otherwise be painful and hard to manage. In the novel, consumption short-circuits whatever grief the family members might feel for the death of the mother, and it assuages the guilt Darl's brothers and sister would otherwise feel for turning their brother in to the authorities. Consumption reconstitutes the family as a whole when its members are in fact an assemblage of uncommunicative individuals, and it intervenes between the youngest child's desire to know why his mother died and the family's inability to offer an explanation.

"Wouldn't you rather have bananas?": this is the only response Vardaman ever gets for his confused reasoning and lack of understanding about his mother's death. Actually, Vardaman would rather have the shiny red electric train he saw one Christmas in a Jefferson store window. Because Vardaman associates Jefferson with the electric train, his mother's death and the plan to bury her in town come to be equated with the train, not the bananas his sister keeps pushing on him. What Dewey Dell understands, but Vardaman cannot yet know, is that neither of her brother's desires will be met and that bananas will be the convenient substitute both for the unattainable answers and the unaffordable electric train (which, in Faulkner's text, represents a different and unattainable social class). Vardaman's experience, while specific to his place in history and social class, can be generalized to almost all children conditioned by capitalism in the First World.

That is, the child's introduction to economics occurs at the level of consumption rather than production. This is very different from the situation earlier in this century, which Vardaman, the child of share-croppers, embodies but no longer represents as the novel progresses.

Vardaman's introduction to commodities demonstrates another dimension of Faulkner's understanding of their fundamental nature. Vardaman learns that one commodity can be readily substituted for another. "Wouldn't you rather have bananas?" Of course an electric train and a bunch of bananas have absolutely nothing in common except as commodities. How might we explain the substitution of one seemingly different commodity for another? The answer has to do with the relational nature of the two forms of value present in the commodity. The substitution of one commodity for another is only possible as use value recedes in relation to exchange value. The fact that Vardaman's desire might be satisfied by a banana speaks for a very different relationship to commodities than one finds in the first chapter of *Capital*, where Marx defines commodities with specifically identifiable use values, such as coats and linen, which are consumed according to wants and needs. These last two terms raise another problem for understanding the commodity as we know it, and that is the relationship of use value to concrete needs on the one hand and on the other its relation to more ephemeral emotional and libidinal desires. Sitting in a buckboard eating bananas, Vardaman is not satisfying a need for food or for potassium. Rather, he is filling in the gaps of his understanding and softening the hurt of his soul. The banana as a commodity clearly has use value, but we are dealing with the economics of desire.

I should like to return to the three commodities, which, like some miraculous answer to a cargo cult's prayers, all but fall out of the blue to put an end to the novel and its family's ordeal. The commodities include a set of false teeth, a graphophone, and the bananas. None is gratuitous as each underscores a current trend in commodity consumption.

For Faulkner's sharecroppers, the bananas represent luxury consumption, not the commonplace fruits they have become for us. Instead, they are the exotic, the tropical, the equivalent of kiwi fruit and cactus apples in our supermarkets today. The transition from the exotic to the commonplace traces the history of most commodities in a society where abundance means surplus. Commodities are introduced as new and forever afterwards must repeat the moment of newness even if it is the same old laundry detergent, packaged in a new box and endowed with a new "fresh scent." Newness ensures that consumption will be a unique experience, will in fact have the power to compensate loss. But because bananas cannot be newly packaged or squirted with a new fresh scent, the preservation of uniqueness requires a constant supply of tropical peculiarities – which in the final analysis signify, both for us and for Faulkner, the Third World.

The reference is crucial for our reading of the novel. As Faulkner portrays it, this particular sharecropping family is as expendable as the entire system of tenant farming had become by the 1930s. In a larger sense, all small-scale agricultural production for the market has no place in the twentieth-century First World state. The current plight of farmers in the Midwest is a culmination of economic patterns which Faulkner discerned in the rural South in the twenties and thirties, whose final outcome will be the massification of agribusiness in the First World and the shift of much agricultural production to the Third World. The Bundren family, perched in their buckboard and eating their way through a bag of bananas, defines an economics whose components include their own demise as producers and re-integration as consumers. From Chilean peaches and nectarines, which have become acceptable wintertime equivalents for our own more readily available pears and apples, right down to the ordinary banana, the Third World is no longer perceived as the distant supplier of *exotic* commodities, but is instead a cornucopia spilling out a steady supply of ordinary foodstuffs for North America's super-markets.

The family's other two commodity acquisitions are just as socially meaningful as the bananas. Take Anse's false teeth, which he claims he needs in order to eat the "victuals God intended a man to eat," but which we know he bought for cosmetic purposes. This is the solution offered by commodity culture for the masculinity Anse felt he lacked when he could not chew meat. As Jewel puts it, "'He got them teeth.' It was a fact. It made him look a foot taller, kind of holding his head up, hangdog and proud too." With the teeth, Anse buys an appearance. In fact, the description of Anse before and after the false teeth summons up magazine advertisements for diet pills and make-up which feature before and after photos of overweight, now slim dieters; or ugly, now beautiful Revlon users. The success of Anse's cosmetic transformation is evident as he rejoins his family, new teeth installed and new wife in tow. In a commodified society, cosmetics evoke sexuality and gratification is synonymous with consumption.

What is interesting about Anse's new wife is the scant attention his children pay to her and the much greater interest they show for her graphophone: the novel's third commodity, packed up in its carrying case and on its way to becoming a household entertainment center. This is a family, mind you, whose members Faulkner has shown absolutely unable to communicate, each locked in awful isolation so that the household is composed of a collection of atomized monads. While all have profound thoughts and long desperately to share them with each other, no one ever says anything beyond the mere exchange of information. I think this is a very modern representation of the American family: Dewey Dell, teenage and pregnant, unable to find the moment or means to confide in another family member; Jewel, secretly moonlighting to get the money to buy a horse (the rural twenties' equivalent of a car); Darl, painting pictures with his mind's eye which for want of paper and paint will never be seen by anyone else; Vardaman, still a child, with no way to put his questions and no one to put them to. The problem, as Faulkner sees it, is not how to establish communication, but how to fill in for its lack. The graphophone, like today's VCR, is the answer: "every time a new record would come from the mail order and us setting in the house in the winter listening to it, I would think what a shame Darl couldn't be to enjoy it too." We can envision the family made round and whole by the addition of the graphophone, its absent members referred to in fondness and soothingly replaced by the music. It is a family unit that need never confront its lack of cohesion and tension-fraught relations because the steady flow of mail-order records sets the rhythm of their daily life.

THE BANANA TODAY: TRIPPING THROUGH LOGOLAND

It is not gratuitous that shopping in a modern chain-store supermarket begins with the fruit and vegetable section. Stepping through the automatic sliding door and leaving behind a dreadful winter slush or blowing cold, you pick up your shopping cart and proceed along the prescribed course which invariably leads to the Land of Oz: a wonderland of brightly colored fruits (first) and vegetables (brown-skinned potatoes last). The produce department offers a striking contrast to the grim realities of congested parking lot and hostile weather. Of course, summertime in the most highly evolved supermarkets can lead to a case of pneumonia, as the temperature inside is always the same frigid 55°F. Winter clothing rather than shorts and a

T-shirt is the most appropriate attire for a trip to the supermarket. If you have ever been uncomfortably cold in the supermarket, found yourself longing for a sweater and hurrying to complete your shopping before turning blue, you may be interested to learn that there is an economic explanation for your discomfort. While a longer stay might mean more purchases, the store's primary economic consideration is not how to attain maximum commodity consumption, but how to minimize the price of energy consumption. The store is overcooled because it costs less to run the air-conditioning at peak than to crank up the four aisles of freezers dispensing Swanson's frozen bounty. The most modern supermarkets have abandoned the old-style freezer chests which opened at the top and were thus more energy efficient (because, as everyone knows, cold air settles and does not tend to escape out of the top of a freezer). These have been replaced by 7-foot-tall, front-opening frozen food display cases, which allow immense quantities of cold air to escape every time the door is opened. Consistent with the illogic of capitalism, stores have opted for air-conditioning as a way of keeping costs down. If you think this is all quite ludicrous, then you have not taken account of the value of display – four or more aisles of 7-foot-high, standing, glass-doored freezer units, containing pies and peas arranged neatly on shelves rather than piled up and buried in the old-style chests.

From the point of view of marketing and cost-cutting, the cold makes sense, but, as I mentioned in chapter 1, I tend to think it also reproduces certain First World ideological associations, particularly in relation to the produce department, where we encounter the agricultural production of sunnier climes. From southern California and Florida to the tropical zones of Mexico, Central America, Colombia, and Ecuador, the produce department features the fruits of the Third World, whose only acceptable attribute of tropicality is color. This is heightened by the use of waxes and, in the most modern supermarkets, the installation of special ceiling lights which make everything, from the peaches to the shoppers, appear orange. Maintained in a constant bath of refrigerated air, these fruits are incapable of producing scents, harboring bugs, growing molds, and becoming decayed. Air-conditioning is a medium of abstraction which severs the agricultural production of the Third World from the heat of labor and the heat of the marketplace. Air-conditioning is a form of packaging. It swaddles the product in First World antiseptic purity and severs its connection with the site of its production. The shopper who enters the air-conditioned supermarket and chooses between its papayas, mangos, pineapples, bananas; its winter supply of peaches, nectarines, plums, and grapes from Chile, is as unaware of the factors and labor force behind their production as the tourist whose experience of Mexico is an air-conditioned hotel lobby.

To grasp that in the First World production is indeed abstracted from consumption, we have only to consider the banana once more and particularly the stickers that festoon the bunches on supermarket counters. Of all the fruits marketed in today's supermarkets, the banana is the least interesting. Always available and cheap, it is now taken for granted. While we might linger over the apples and oranges in an attempt to choose between different sizes and varieties (do we want Florida or California; Washington State or Appalachia?), the banana fails to stimulate such questions. First of all, while there are countless varieties of native bananas, distinguished by their taste, texture, and color, the North American palate has been trained to accept only one: the Lacatan. Plantains and small red bananas are sometimes marketed along with the more recognizable yellow variety. But these seem of a different class altogether. The choice does not seem one of choosing between a Granny Smith and a Red Delicious, but between a banana and something else. While a supermarket can hardly consider itself "super" without bananas, the status of its produce department depends upon the availability and appearance of everything besides bananas. No longer the exotic commodity, the unique and satisfying object of consumption described in Faulkner's novel, the banana is commonplace and bought out of habit. There it is – green or yellow; winter, spring, summer, or fall – about the only thing that distinguishes one banana from another is its sticker. I would like to focus on these small adhesive patches, for they are as suggestive of our relationship to commodities today as the banana itself was in Faulkner's novel.

In a society defined by consumption, where the commodity is perceived as separate from its site, moment, and mode of production, commodities seem to offer themselves up spontaneously to the consumer. Have you noticed how bananas are displayed? – mounded or ranked in rows, their yellow and preferably unmarred skins spotted with brightly colored stickers. In the absence of any clues as to how the bananas were grown, how they were packaged and shipped, how they were then marketed and distributed, finally, whose hands and labor brought them from plantation to supermarket, the logo seems to

offer itself as some sort of explanation. It suggests that the multinational made each banana possible. The logo is emblematic of production without revealing anything specific about production. We have
all chuckled over the plight of the small child who has to be taught
that milk comes from cows and is not simply produced in and
packaged by the supermarket. Commodity consumption is structured
in such a way that we are all put in the position of the child. While we
are told that cows make milk and bananas grow on trees, biological
simplicity belies the complex reality of the highly rationalized system
of production defined by multinational capitalism. The multinational
is distant and unknowable while its logo is concrete and visible. This
is the topsy-turvy logic of capitalism which promotes and depends
upon a naive consumer.

Currently, banana-sticker logos include a reference to the Latin
American nation of their origin: Chiquita Costa Rica, Del Monte
Columbia, Ecuador Turbana. This is a departure from earlier designs
which gave only the company name. I have the feeling that the
inclusion of country name represents a ploy to suggest diversification
on the part of the company or some meaningless recognition of the
autonomy of local governments. In any case, the abstract design of the
logo combined with the already separate and alien environment of the
supermarket makes less real the site of production as an actual place
complete with a history and a people. The nation, reduced to its
name, becomes a part of a catchy title: Chiquita Costa Rica, whose
syncopated effect is the welding of country to corporations.

Because production is encapsulated in the logo, stuck on the
banana and included in its purchase and peeling, the notion of
production becomes, for the consumer, a feature of consumption.
Today I am eating a Colombian banana, tomorrow I might have one
from Costa Rica! The name creates the illusion of difference at the
level of consumption, which, given the uniformity of the mass-
produced product, would otherwise be unremarkable. In this way,
the consumer never has to confront real difference, which is located in
production, where it is defined by one multinational's policies and
history in relation to a particular nation, its politics and workforce.
The control of production and marketing by multinationals heightens
the fantastic quality of commodity fetishism. If, as Marx defined
them, commodities are the containers of hidden social relationships,
certainly these social relationships are all the more concealed by the
movement of production to the Third World and the disassociation of
the multinationals from more traditional corporations whose own-

ership policies were part of the public domain. Distancing is both geographic and conceptual. If you are a shareholder in United Brands, then your *Annual Report* will sometimes include a photograph of brown-skinned women happily packing bunches of bananas in plastic bags for shipping. If you are consumer without shares in the company, all you will see is the "Chiquita Senorita," diminutive and smiling, the logo's fetishized portrayal of the workforce. Actually, the publicity photograph, which cuts a segment out of the production line and focuses on a couple of uniformed employees, all neatly packaged by the photograph's glossy finish, is no less ideological than the folkloric banana sticker version.

A sampling of banana logos demonstrates their high degree of abstract stylization. The name of the multinational is all that matters, except in the case of United Fruit Company, whose involvement in the overthrow of the Arbenz government of Guatemala (Schlesinger and Kinzer, 1983) makes it preferable to front the Chiquita label. For reasons I will develop shortly, I think it would be wrong to consider corporate names such as Dole and Del Monte as brand names. These are instead the insignia of multinationals, complete and autonomous in themselves. As such, they signify much more than brands. If the logos are predominantly graphic abstractions, they allow the consumer to interpret them according to his or her fantasies. Ecuador Turbana might suggest a tropical sunset seen through the jalousies. Many interpretations are possible, all fed by our ideologized travel brochure images of the tropics. The only outstanding graphic feature, which needs no interpretation, is the name of the multinational. Here referent and representation are one.

The Chiquita sticker is the only logo that harks back to a previous, less abstract and more figural era in advertising. It features a tiny banana sporting Carmen Miranda hat and flouncy dancing-costume sleeves. As one of the first companies to use banana-sticker logos, United Brands was already planning a media campaign in 1973 based on nostalgia for the Chiquita figure. In consumer society, traditions are born overnight and endowed with nostalgia as a feature of their creation. In any case, the folkloric emblem, reminiscent of Disney's "Tres Caballeros" cartoon, effectively masks the modern, highly technologized multinational which also markets A & W Rootbeer, Baskin-Robbins 31 Flavors ice-cream, and Morrell meat products.

For the most part logos eschew figural representations. This is what separates them from older-style advertising associated with brand names. I would suggest that the big difference between brand names and logos (the former associated with specific products; the latter signifying the corporation), which can also be discerned at the level of format and design (the brand-name insignia, figural and representative; the logo, abstract, broadly interpretive, but not representational) may articulate at another level what some economists have suggested is a transformation in capitalism itself. Indeed, we might make a case for some fundamental change in capitalism by citing the very different nature of traditional nineteenth-century capitalism typified by entrepreneurial figures such as Henry Ford, or the older icons of American capitalism: Rockefeller and Vanderbilt; as compared to late twentieth-century capitalist society, where the relationships of both production and consumption no longer have the direct, unmediated quality we felt them to have when bosses were bosses and workers clearly contracted with them for the sale of their labor power.

LEARNING FROM MICKEY: THE EVOLUTION OF THE LOGO

Although economists will probably disapprove, I am going to focus more closely on consumption, rather than production, to demonstrate something about the lived experience of late twentieth-century capitalism. In so doing, I recognize that most consumers are also producers, and that we ought to be able to talk about capitalism as a whole. But one of the features of our society is that we tend to live production and consumption as completely separate activities. In working towards a more profound analysis of consumption, I hope to offer a means of understanding how our lives as consumers and workers are, in fact, related. To do so, I will turn to a figure whose history is longer than the Chiquita Senorita. I am referring to Mickey Mouse, whose evolution as an icon of popular culture extends from the thirties to the nineties and offers what may be the only example of the step-by-step development of the logo, which I take as symptomatic of changes happening in consumption and within capitalism as a whole.

As is well known, Mickey Mouse was first defined as a character in animated cartoons. Soon afterwards, and through the agency of merchandising, however, Mickey stepped out of the purely characterological mode and lent himself to a number of emblematic reproduction – his body reworked and sold as dolls, his shape and features traced upon dishes, cups, and watches. A brief survey of the commod-

Photo: Karen Klugman

ities available in the thirties reveals not only a tremendous number of Disney-inspired items, but a generalized practice whereby the characters defined in the media were used as emblems to promote the sale of merchandise. It is quite clear that the impetus of merchandising breaks up and reshuffles all the categories we tend to think of as separate in the field of popular culture – movies; music; decor – making it possible for Popeye to decorate table clocks and cookie jars to be made in the image of Aunt Jemima. I want to stress that the reshuffling of genres involves much more than the use of icons for decoration. With the purchase of a 1933 Emerson table radio whose sides depict Mickey Mouse playing a variety of musical instruments, the consumer bought into all of popular culture. This is possible because Mickey is being used as a signifier. So, then, the transformation from cartoon character to emblem occurs with the definition of a commodity. Then, as these commodities and their emblems become more familiar, yet another transformation is produced: from emblem to sign. I would say that Mickey Mouse definitely becomes a sign when he is no longer depicted as a complete (and very rat-like) body, but is instead reduced to the shorthand of large bright eyes and saucer-shaped ears. This stage is clearly reached in the fifties with the Mickey Mouse Club TV show, whose Mousekateers popularized the famous Mickey hats, consisting of not much more than big ears. The sign as an abstraction, makes possible an even wider diffusion of commodities, whose consumption no longer depends upon an actual purchase, but may be achieved while watching TV.

The possibility of a purely visual mode of consumption brings us to the logo. If you have ever been to Disneyland in California, then you have seen the Mickey Mouse flowerbed. This is one of the world's most remarkable logos. There, just as you enter the park, on a raised embankment where it is traced and colored in pansies and marigolds, is the gigantic smiling face of Mickey Mouse. This logo absolutely transcends the relationship to specific commodities, leaving only its visual consumption as a sign, which grants the consumer not only all of Disneyland and Walt Disney Enterprises, but all of popular culture as well. It is important to note that the visitor's consumption of the Mickey Mouse logo occurs while walking towards and into Disneyland. To understand the crucial connection between the logo, its visual apprehension, and the consumer's mobility, I would like to unpack the logo and show how it works.

To do so, I will refer to another aspect of Disneyland which has to do precisely with its ability to create different historical and geographic settings in each of its five lands. Actually, Disneyland is the best example of a text and the features that comprise it. Real histories and places are of no concern at Disneyland; rather, it is assembled out of all the signifying bits already defined within the terrain of popular culture as references of time and place, but emptied of real history. The best word I know to describe the process of putting texts together is "theming." Each of Disneyland's worlds uses a combination of visual and auditory stimuli to enact a specific theme. For example,

everything in Frontierland, from the log fort and Dodge City storefronts to the costumes of the shopkeepers, dance-hall girls and river pilots, suggests the popularized version of the Wild West. Theming re-creates in geographic space the same sort of effect produced in the movie theater; that is, it evokes a closed world and draws the viewer (that is, the visitor) into it. Indeed, the great movie theaters of the thirties were theme palaces, the fanciful architecture and exotic decor of which evoked foreign lands, such as Egypt and the Orient, or heavenly natural settings, with ceilings painted in stars and hung with clouds. At Disneyland, besides architecture, decor and costumery, music and other recorded messages – even food – are used to produce themes. These are then activated in relation to the visitor's movement either on a particular ride or at random about the park. Commentators have remarked on the importance of movement in Disneyland both as a consequence of having to get 40,000 people a day through the park and as a symptom of Los Angeles itself, where daily life is conducted behind the wheel of a car (Birman, 1979). But I would argue that the significance of movement goes beyond the necessary and symptomatic and resides finally in the way theming is constituted, through movement, as a narrative.

At Disneyland, theming is most successful when the narratives are highly controlled and tightly organized, as they are in the park's most memorable ride: "The Pirates of the Caribbean." The ride commences as you board a pirate long-boat amidst an evening bayou setting complete with fireflies and riverfront shacks. Very quickly the adventure begins, as you plummet down a water-slide into the world of the pirates and the past. This part of the ride includes the capture of New Orleans, the auctioning-off of the town's women, and a final drunken revel whose outcome can only be the complete destruction of the city. Luckily, at this point you magically ascend out of the world of the pirates, and return to the bayou evening where the ride ends. Throughout, you have been a participant in the ride, stringing together its sequence of events as you move through space, thus constituting a narrative.

The notion of theming rejoins the definition of the logo; for the logo represents a highly condensed form of theming. It pulls together what in Disneyland's environments is a vast array of thematic material, dispenses with the narrative glue and gives the consumer everything in one eyeful. Motion, however, is still essential. As we walk past the Mickey Mouse flowerbed, drive along the highway, or push a cart up and down the aisles of a supermarket, we consume logos, stringing them together in the larger narratives of everyday life. To underscore the necessary relationship between logos and the consumer's mobility, I call to your attention the first use of logos: the insignias developed by the oil companies to designate their gas stations: the Texaco star, Mobil's flying red horse. Dating from the twenties and thirties, these very quickly became synonymous with highway travel, and were intended to be perceived by mobile consumers (who, whether or not they stopped for gas, would still have consumed the company's sign).

From this point of view, the motorist and shopper, just like the Disneyland visitor, are passive theme builders and logo collectors – not narrators, but instruments of the narration. I would like to give one more example of our relationship to commodity consumption as this is defined by the logo. To do so, I will refer to an omnipresent fast-food chain: McDonald's, whose logo, the golden arches, litters the landscape in more ways than one. Once under the sign of the logo, the consumer's behavior is so highly determined that it need not be directed. To illustrate, instead of mentioning the menu selections or the waiting in line, I would like to comment upon the "Thank You" inscribed above the McDonald's trash containers. This is very different from the "Push" found on public trash cans out on the sidewalk. The "Thank You" dispenses with the customer's choice and assumes a prescribed mode of behavior even as the customer walks in the door, before he or she has bought anything let alone thought about throwing it away. In contrast, out on the street the choice to litter or not is up to the individual. "Push" constitutes a directive for the trash can's use but does not prescribe behavior. In a world defined by the logo, we can no longer talk about coercion, control, or those other nasty epithets leveled at the advertising industry, whose goal was to get people to buy certain brand-name products. Under the sign of the logo consumption is assured; the choice between various brand names superseded by the flow of commodities.

"Go with the flow" is an expression which circulated widely in California surfing culture a year or two ago. I think it best sums up the notion of advanced consumer society as it has been portrayed in the work of contemporary French theorists such as Guy Debord (1977) and Baudrillard (1970). What typifies their writing is the image of a society in which consumers and commodities seem to circulate freely and endlessly in a fantastic democracy of consumption. Herein lies the great fallacy of late capitalism. Obviously, we do not all share equally in commodities nor do we even have equal opportunity to trade evenly in their signs – not racial minorities, not the unemployed, not women, children, teenagers, the elderly, not the populations of the Third World. In fact, taken to the logical extreme, the very notion of universalized consumption defined largely upon the visual apprehension of logos, would, in a very short time, produce a society of disenchanted "hunger artists."

This is the ideology of consumer society whose internal logic reveals the fundamental contradiction of capitalism. It is a contradiction already apparent when Faulkner wrote depicting a population who might function as consumers without at the same time being producers. The fact that he can portray such an untenable situation, which is then perceived as normal (certainly no one else has raised this issue), tells us something about our own time. If people are more apt to think of themselves as consumers rather than producers, if gratification is associated with consumption rather than working, doing, and making, we have only to bear in mind that this is a society where work is either unattainable or alienating. The contradictions we identify at the level of consumption are in fact the contradictions of production.

The notion of democratized consumption comes into being as labor is devalued and the workforce is removed from the scene. If I have cited Disneyland and McDonald's, it is because amusements and fast

59

Photo: Karen Klugman

food typify the way in which production is perceived in a commodified society. At Disneyland, workers are referred to as actors, made to wear costumes and transform their labor into roles. At McDonald's work is trivialized. Rather than being regarded as producers, the employees are seen as burger assemblers.

The possibility of a purely visual mode of consumption, wherein consumers need not buy a product in order to apprehend the universalized notion of the multinational, occurs as the logo becomes essentialized in relation to the de-essentialization of the commodity itself. This is possible as use value wanes in relation to exchange value. Use value comes into question and diminishes in importance when goods appear to be spontaneously produced, as they do when assembled on supermarket and department-store counters, awaiting the "first touch" of the consumer. The notion of spontaneous production bespeaks the erasure of the workforce, separated by distance and severed from the site of commodity consumption by the system of multinational production.

The contradictions of consumption are the contradictions of production. Because the lived experience of capitalism in the First World state prioritizes consumption over production, we can begin to think critically about our relationship to capitalism by scrutinizing our relationship to commodities.

BACKGROUND SOURCES AND
FURTHER READING

Given his importance in the formation of mass culture, Walt Disney, as an object of critical study, has been greatly neglected. Few studies attempt to evaluate the ideological and utopian impulses in his work.

Marin, Louis (1977) "Disneyland: a degenerate utopia," *Glyph* I.
Willis, Susan (1987) "Fantasia: Walt Disney's Los Angeles suite," *Diacritics* 17: 83–96.
Wilson, Alexander (1985) "The managed landscape: the organization of Disney World," *Impulse*, summer: 22–5.
——(1986) "The betrayal of the future," *Socialist Review* 15: 41–54.

4

WORK(ING) OUT

OUR BODIES, OURSELVES

In 1971 the Boston Women's Health Book Collective published a resource book for women that represented a significant victory in the struggle waged by women for autonomy. The book, *Our Bodies, Ourselves*, was extremely visible throughout the early seventies. Its dog-eared, paper-bound cover featuring a photograph of banner-waving women could be found in many women's homes, on the sofa or kitchen counter, where it served as a focal point to rally women's desire for collective activity, discussion, and a full range of "consciousness-raising" pursuits. I mention this book because, seen now in retrospect, it clearly defines an important moment in the Women's Movement of this century, one whose political specificity no longer exists, but one that we need to remember in order to understand the problems we must face in the last decade of the twentieth century if the struggle for liberation is to continue.

I rediscovered *Our Bodies, Ourselves* just the other day, ran across it on an undistinguished shelf at the public library and flipped through its pages to review the photos, essays, and testimony. I was deeply struck by the dramatic simplicity of the book's conceptualization both of selfhood and of struggle. Ours is not an era that offers such direct, bold, and concrete statements and strategies to women. I want to cite two of the book's testimonies because they so clearly define the collective's goals and the opposition its members faced. The first testimony is that of a young mother whose voice, like that of all the testimonies assembled in the book, combines with the observations and assessments made by the collective and demonstrates the collective's desire to develop a non-centered, and therefore non-authoritarian discourse:

I watch my daughter. From morning to night her body is her home. She lives in it and with it. When she runs around the kitchen she uses all of herself. Every muscle in her body moves when she laughs, when she cries. When she rubs her vulva, there is no awkwardness, no feeling that what she is doing is wrong. She feels pleasure and expresses it without hesitation. She knows when she wants to be touched and when she wants to be left alone. She doesn't have to think about it – it's a very direct physical asking or responding to someone else. It's beautiful to be with her. I sometimes feel she is more a model for me than I am for her! Occasionally I feel jealous of the ease with which she lives inside her skin. I want to be a child again! It's so hard to get back that sense of body as home.

(Boston Women's Health Book Collective, 1976: 40)

There is something very appealing about the organic construction of selfhood: the body as home for the self. By comparison with the way in which contemporary feminists confront women's experience of alienation and sense of inferiority by focusing on ever more narrowly defined problems such as sexuality, which is then subdivided by sexual preference and scrutinized in relation to linguistic and psychoanalytic theories; or women's roles as these are stratified by capitalism and shaped by male domination; or women's image, as this has been generated by the media and defined by the all-powerful "male gaze," *Our Bodies, Ourselves* boldly ties everything up in a holistic struggle where selfhood emerges as women learn to take care and control of their bodies.

The primary reason why the Boston collective saw their struggle so clearly and completely is the unmediated male domination of health care which they confronted and contested. Moreover, the generally polarized nature of late sixties politics combined with more overt forms of male domination in all sectors of society than women today can ever expect to confront, produced a situation in which women could grasp their struggle against overt oppression, in which they could define specific goals and at the same time see themselves bound up in a larger collective quest for wholeness and affirmation.

Read in hindsight, the book's documentation of unmitigated misogyny is starkly appalling. However, such hostility can have an explosively invigorating effect because it offers women a clear target against which they can define oppositional attitudes and strategies. Witness this horrifying statement by a male gynecologist:

total hysterectomy should also be performed as prophylactic procedure. Under these circumstances, the uterus becomes a useless, bleeding, symptom-producing, potentially cancer-bearing organ and therefore should be removed . . . To sterilize a woman and allow her to keep a useless and potentially lethal organ is incompatible with modern gynecological concepts. Hysterectomy is the only logical approach to surgical steriliza-tion of women.

(Boston Women's Health Book Collective, 1976: 148)

This doctor's disgust for the bodies of his patients renders visible the ideological supports of male domination against which women shaped their struggles throughout the sixties and early seventies in unequivocal terms. The project defined by the Boston Women's Health Book Collective is compassionately to demonstrate that women's struggle for autonomy requires wresting control over their bodies away from male-dominated medical practice and phar-maceutical industry. Their book makes it clear that ignorance is a barrier to selfhood and a tool for domination. Liberation means becoming familiar with the body, exploring it, particularly the sexual-ly taboo zones, in order to seize the body as the site for the definition of self in community.

Today, nothing is the same. The notion of political wholeness that shaped so many women's collectives and projects has evaporated, as has the possibility of conceptualizing autonomy as a basic, well-nigh organic, unity. If anything, women's struggle has become diffuse and rendered all the more frustrating for the lack of sharply drawn male opposition. This is not to say that male domination no longer exists to serve the interests of capitalism. Our society is still a male-dominated one. But the forms of domination are less recognizable. In many daily-life situations patriarchy is part and parcel with commodity culture and commodity gratification. One of the aims of this chapter is to disengage instances of domination from commodified practice, thus rendering it in stark detail and triggering women's impulse for oppositionality and alternative thinking. Women's bodies are still a contested zone. Although the terms of the struggle have shifted since the sixties, many women continue to situate their primary desire for liberation in a bodily expression of selfhood. To understand how male domination intersects today with women's bodily articulation of selfhood, I would shift the analysis from the unmediated forms of domination we find in health care to the amorphous, highly mediated realm of daily life in consumer society, where I would begin by looking at women's exercise programs.

THE WORKOUT

Many young women today do not realize that exercise for women as a widely available and socially acceptable endeavor represents a recent victory in women's struggle for equality with men. Looking back at *Our Bodies, Ourselves*, I was amazed by the book's comparatively mild chapter on exercise. It urges women to get into exercise, investigate a YMCA program, or consider taking up a sport such as swimming, tennis, perhaps jogging. How tame these suggestions seem by comparison to the exercise standards many women set for themselves today. I had forgotten that most of the book's readers would have grown up in an era that downplayed the importance of exercise for women. None of the book's original readers would have benefited from Title IX legislation that opened public-school team sports to girls. One of the positive outgrowths of the Women's Movement in the sixties has been the invigorating of the female body coupled with the acceptability of women appearing in public actively engaged in vigorous physical activity. Sixty-minute aerobics workouts four or five times a week or a jogging program aimed at twenty-five miles a week, these are the exercise standards many women set for themselves. Most are white, middle-class, professional women, although many younger black women students and professionals are beginning to enter the exercise lifestyle. Racial equality and class mobility are synonymous with the professions and professional workouts. For the working class in general, and particularly black women who work outside the home, freedom means liberation from effort: "Why exercise when you kill yourself working all day?"

I want to look at women's exercise, bearing in mind its narrowly defined constituency, but realizing at the same time that middle-class white America defines the model and the look of consumer capitalism. I also want to maintain a sense of all the positive features that exercise for women generates, including the development of independence and the opportunity for bonding between women; but I want particularly to scrutinize the way exercise has evolved in a commodified society so as to contain or limit these positive features.

At the time when the Boston Women's Health Book Collective urged women to sign up for exercise at local recreation halls and YMCAs, many women had begun to make exercise a part of their daily lives with Jack LaLanne. A TV entrepreneur of exercise and health products, LaLanne mixed rhythmic stretching, bouncing, and bending with brazen exhortations to "Bertha" and "Gertie" to get up off their bulgy behinds, work their baggy thighs, and strengthen their flabby underarms. "Come on now, Clara, do just one more." LaLanne's daily half-hour exercise program was immensely popular during the sixties. It underscored a moment when many women found themselves bound up in domestic space and work, with the TV something of a companion during the hours when children and husband were out of the house. LaLanne's exercise had the practical-ity of offering women a wide range of movements that could be performed with no more fancy equipment than a straight-legged wooden chair. Women at the time did not seem to consider the jarring incongruity of shaping their movements to the video image of a very muscled man, whose bulging pectorals and biceps they could not hope to achieve even if they performed every movement ten times as directed. In the early sixties, women who sought autonomy through exercise had to put up with patronizing male attitudes towards women's "lesser" physical capabilities, outright condescension to-wards flab, and exaggerated macho images of male physical prowess. LaLanne is reported to have swum from Alcatraz to the mainland, his hands manacled behind him, and towing a small boat. This may be a figure for liberation, but it is not one any of the male prisoners on Alcatraz ever duplicated, nor is it one the sixties' housewife could readily emulate.

Today LaLanne has been replaced by a new male TV guru of exercise for women: Richard Simmons, who was once proportioned like the Pillsbury Dough Boy and now offers his slimmer, trimmer body as an example of what every overweight woman can achieve. With a round baby face and somewhat childish voice, Simmons offers women a lot less machismo than LaLanne but he serves up equal doses of condescension towards flab. Where LaLanne aggressively chided women for being overweight, Simmons cajoles and preaches. Of course, neither one ever mentions that male domination, which restricts many women to homelife or body-restricting clerical jobs, is a major flab-producing factor. Both LaLanne and Simmons define the woman viewer as offensive to the male gaze and helpless – if not altogether mindless – for having allowed her body to become too large in the first place.

In the face of overt male domination of exercise for women, Jane Fonda's *Workout*, and particularly her "Prime time workout" for women in midlife, represent something of a feminist alternative in the exercise market. Published in 1981, the *Workout* book was in the bestseller charts for two years and continues to be newly discovered and widely read by women. Its diffusion has subsequently been extended by a videotape version available in every home video rental store. In her forties when the book first appeared, with photographs of herself throughout, Fonda undertook the task of "womanizing" exercise. She made it clear that women of all ages could strive for and attain health, strength, and a good-looking body (although many women drew the line at doing back flips *à la* Fonda).

The "Prime time workout" included in the book of essays *Women Coming of Age*, is an excellent model for understanding how far a feminist approach to exercise can go in a culture that continues to be defined by men and capitalism. I see the whole book as an exercise in contradiction whose tentative towards defining women-centered notions about the female body bring to light in equal measure the limitations our society places on the full realization of such alternatives. The title "Prime time workout" is a good case in point. Fonda explains her choice of words by underscoring the double meaning of prime time. A woman's "prime of life" – her middle years – elides with the notion of network prime time. Fonda makes the comparison in order to emphasize a simple point about sexism. That is, men in their prime times are like the 9:00 p.m. slot on CBS. They are the most sought after, most successful, most esteemed. In contrast, women at age 40 are made to feel like a 4:00 sit-com rerun (a.m. or p.m., take your pick).

The book is written to stake women's claim on the future and on future definitions of womanhood. But as Fonda explains in her introduction, *Women Coming of Age* documents a moment of transition. It is not yet clear to Fonda writing the book or any of us following its guidelines what sort of women will emerge as the eighties and post-eighties come to be defined more and more by women over 40 in the workforce and in the public eye. The problem Fonda confronts is how to shape the transition, deeply burdened as she is with twentieth-century male dominated ideas of womanhood, where beauty is synonymous with youth. Proclaiming that the physical characteristics of a woman's aging are "negotiable" (Fonda, 1984: 39), Fonda defines a thin line between recapitulating the quest for beauty (how to combat facial wrinkles, for instance) and affirming some wholly new and autonomous notion of womanhood whose precursors are the 50-year-old marathon-runners and swimmers whose photographs

Hot.

Smooth. Brilliant. A superior burn.

Eagle Fitness Systems.
By Cybex, the leader in sports
medicine technology.

EAGLE

crop up throughout the book and function as reality principles to the more glamorous dance-pose photographs of Fonda herself.

Because I read *Women Coming of Age* after having rediscovered *Our Bodies, Ourselves*, I could not help but read Fonda's book in the light of the early seventies' project. Because many women currently in their prime times have the sixties embedded in their life experience, this is perhaps not an inappropriate way to consider Fonda's book. From this perspective, the question of selfhood that informs the earlier project is everywhere implicated in Fonda's writing but nowhere confronted. Indeed, Fonda comes across as something of a collective in one as the book features photographs of Fonda, like so many stills from her movies, defining her now as child, now mother, or wife, now camp counselor, or researcher, and finally pet-keeper. All of these roles are finally subsumed by the "I" of Fonda, the book's narrator, who speaks from experience and with great conviction. Residual traces of collective social practice enter Fonda's writing in other ways. There is the workout group itself, and the testimonies of women who have benefited from Fonda's program. Some, we are told, have been active politically both in the United Farm Workers Movement and the Campaign for Economic Democracy. However, the emergence of selfhood and the sense of collective activity are both cut short and contained by the book's narrow focus on bodily wellbeing, which is defined specifically as a product of the workout.

This brings me to a consideration of the other half of the "Prime time workout" title: the notion of the "workout" itself. My hypothesis is that the workout, as the contradictory synthesis of work and leisure, may well represent the most highly evolved commodity form yet to appear in late twentieth-century consumer capitalism. The workout isolates the individual for the optimal expenditure of selectively focused effort aimed at the production of the quintessential body object. Nevertheless, I would maintain that the workout, and particularly the nautilus workout, includes utopian dimensions as well. In seeking to reveal how the workout embodies production and consumption in capitalist society and the desire for their utopian transformation, I am elaborating on Frederic Jameson's dictum that: "even the most degraded type of mass culture has a [utopian dimension] which remains implicitly, and no matter how faintly, critical of the social order from which (as a commodity) it springs" (Jameson, 1979: 144).

The workout represents the culmination of the trend in exercise towards privatization. The process originates at the turn of the century with "males only" health clubs and terminates in today's unisex exercise spas. It is abundantly clear that exercise is a commodity with the advent of TV exercise shows and the now more individualized mode of consumption: the videocassette. In today's big money exercise market, the only possible antithesis to the commodity form is the local community exercise class offered in school gymnasiums or church recreation halls. However, the burgeoning of glitzy private clubs and spas has made YMCA and community recreation programs appear lackluster and old-fashioned – something for the elderly and middle-age-spread cases. The difference between a workout in a private spa and an exercise class at the "Y" is the way the latter promotes bonding between women and a sense of community that cuts across the generations and socio-economic strata. Women who participate in community-organized programs generally comment that they most appreciate getting to know, and to laugh and sweat with other women. Community-sponsored exercise programs do not sever their participants from their lives with families and friends. Rather, the exercise class creates an opportunity for women to develop themselves in community with other women. Such opportunities are absolutely negated when exercise is channeled by the media into private living-rooms. The private spa, then, offers escape from job or domestic space, but it severely limits the opportunities for conversation and community. This is because a woman who participates in aerobics at a spa is made to see herself as an isolated individual. The atmosphere of the spa promotes an aura of body rivalry. Mirrors are everywhere. Women compare but do not share themselves with others. They see themselves as bodies. They scrutinize their lines and curves and they check out who is wearing the hottest leotard.

The workout focuses women's positive desires for strength, agility, and the physical affirmation of self and transforms these into competition over style and rivalry for a particular body look and performance. Body rivalry has long been a feature of men's exercise. Men flexing for themselves and each other in front of a mirror is the single most expressive metaphor of masculinity and exercise. The workout puts women in contention with one another for the right look. For women, poised body line and flexed muscles are only half the picture. Achieving the proper workout look requires several exercise costumes, special no-smudge make-up, and an artfully understated hair-do.

The workout produces the gendered look of exercise: long Barbie-doll legs, strikingly accentuated by iridescent hot pink tights, offset by

wearing "Shape-Ups" (1970).

By permission of Mattel UK Ltd

a pair of not too floppy purple leg-warmers (worn even when the weather is warm); a willowy body poured into a plum-colored leotard whose leg openings define the thigh at waist level; and finally a color-coordinated headband (or wristbands) – teasing reminders that in order to look the way it does the body must sweat. Many women now wear their exercise costumes while doing errands to and from the spa. I have seen women in dazzling workout costumes on line at McDonald's, getting cash at the bank's instant teller, picking their children up from day care, pushing a shopping cart at the supermarket, and on city streets from coast to coast. Most women who appear in public *à la* exercise choose not to cover up their luminescent body socks with blouse, skirt, or dungarees. In so doing, they unabashedly define themselves as workout women. In making a public body statement, a woman affirms herself as someone who has seized control over the making and shaping of her body. She demonstrates her right to participate in professional body-toning, an endeavour previously felt to be a man's prerogative. However, all these affirmative, apparently liberatory aspects of a woman's public exercise statement are negated by the simple fact that men do not appear in public similarly clad. Why should they? Being male is synonymous with having muscles, just as it is synonymous with having a penis. The workout, notwithstanding its co-ed classes and equal access to the nautilus, substantiates male domination through the gendered look of exercise. As with most things in our society, having gender generally comes to mean being female. By the simple reason of being dominant, men need not proclaim themselves as gendered subjects. Women, who define their struggle for equality solely at the level of gender, stand to gain little more than the right to appear as gendered subjects. The image of the workout woman articulates the fundamental contradiction between the desire for dramatic transformation shackled to the desire for gender identity, in a society where only one gender needs definition.

"Get in Shape, Girl." This refrain gives its name to a line of products and their advertising jingle featuring play exercise accessories for young girls. There are special exercise bangles, leotard belts, and pastel "Heavy hands" for 6- and 7-year-old girls. The message is clear: exercise is a commodity. It is not something you do, but something you buy and wear.

WORKING

Many women who workout today work at managerial jobs, part-time jobs, clerical jobs, micro-assembly jobs, and professional sit-down, body-restricting, stress-producing jobs. For such women the not so distant remembrance of Rosie the Riveter must summon up striking alternative notions of women in the workforce. Rosie the Riveter is an icon intimately associated with industrial labour during the Second World War. Clad in overalls and a hard hat, toting tools and a metal lunch-box, Rosie the Riveter represents the explosive moment when women as a group appropriated not just the uniforms and roles traditionally reserved for men, but actually seized the single most important symbol of male-dominated industrial capitalism: the machine. The image of Rosie the Riveter astride the tremendous fuselage of a B-52 gives feminist reversal to the privileged relationship of man to machine defined a century earlier by Emile Zola in his apocalyptic railroad epic *La Bête Humaine*. Zola's portrayal of the engineer who forces bone, muscle, and passion to control a hurtling locomotive epitomizes man's integral relationship with the machine, unbroken until the 1940s.

Unlike Rosie the Riveter, who dramatically defined women as a productive force, most working women today have difficulty perceiving their labor in terms of production. Many working men also feel disassociated from producing, but the experience is largely a woman's experience because women predominate in service-sector employment as well as in unskilled and micro-assembly jobs. If we were to consider the broad history of women in the workplace from the Second World War to the present, we would begin with women's appropriation of industrial jobs in the forties, their return to domesticity in the fifties, and their re-induction into the labor force during the seventies and eighties as a low-skilled and low-paid component of the labor force. The image of women actively engaged in production and intimately associated with machinery has been erased from popular iconography. Even if she works a forty-hour week, a woman will probably never be thought of as having anything to do with machinery other than labor-saving kitchen devices (like the food processor ironically named "La Machine") and the family car.

In the context of women's labor history, the nautilus machine is a capitalist wish-fulfillment. It gives women access to the machine but denies access to production. It requires energy and effort and negates the experience of labor. It isolates the individual from other women

73

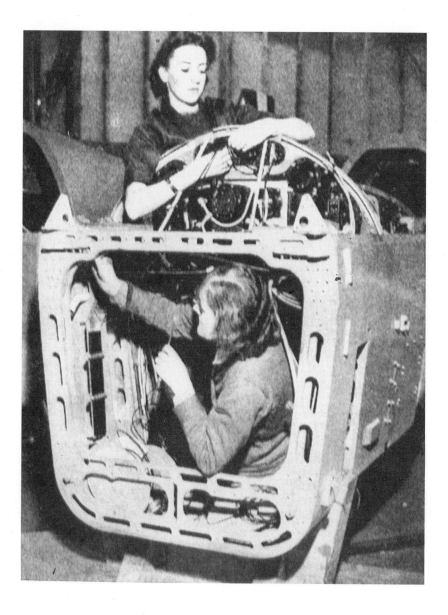

who work out and defines her body as an assemblage of body areas and muscle functions, each requiring a specialized machine and machine function. The nautilus machine and the woman who works out on it is the distorted 1980s equivalent of Rosie the Riveter astride the body of a battleship. As an icon in the popular imagination, the nautilus metaphorizes women's relationship to self and to labor. Nothing is produced but the body itself.

"You practically crawl inside it." This is how my son characterized working out on the nautilus as compared to the now old-fashioned weight-lifting equipment where your strength is pitted against the machine's resistance. When asked to describe the nautilus, most people have expressed similar feelings of being assimilated into the machine. Rather than the direct expenditure of effort out of your body, along a wire, over a pulley to lift a weight, the nautilus incorporates your body into its function. The woman inside the nautilus machine is the object produced by the machine even while she is at the same time the producer producing herself as product of the machine. The allusion to production is enhanced by the layout of the room housing the nautilus. Anyone who has ever visited a machine shop will see in the nautilus' division of labor, where separate machines are designed and situated in order to accomplish specific tasks, a mirrored and chrome version of a tool and die shop.

The woman who works out has the illusive gratification of being in the workplace, where she can experience at first hand the reduction of labor into repetitive, narrowly defined tasks.

What I find most striking about mass culture today is that many of the features that define a particular mass-cultural object, such as those that typify the aerobics workout, are reiterated in other cultural objects, some of them from the realm of "high" art. A good example is the photographic artist Cindy Sherman, whose work has for some time been acclaimed by the New York art world and has more recently come to the attention of the popular press, such as *Vogue* magazine. Cindy Sherman's photography enacts the same relationship to production and consumption as do women who work out on the nautilus machine. The majority of Sherman's photographs are of herself. Most of the earlier work resembles black and white movie stills with Sherman depicted as someone either in a Fellini landscape or a hollywood B-movie. Curiously enough, many of Sherman's photographs bear a strong resemblance to the photographs of Jane Fonda that appear in the movie star's workout books.

Sherman's photographs of herself are not self-portraits in the traditional sense of the term because each photograph reveals an entirely different Cindy Sherman. Each is a discrete photo-object whose singular subject is made-up, costumed, and depicted as somehow autonomous and separate from Cindy Sherman the photographer. Sherman is both the photographer and the subject photographed. She is inside the production/reproduction circuit. She is the product produced and hung on the gallery wall for public consumption and at the same time she is the producer producing the body-image product. There is a famous wood-block print by Albrecht Dürer which many students encounter in an introductory art history course. It depicts a male artist in the process of capturing on paper the reclining figure of a nude female. Between the artist and his subject is a grid, through which the artist gazes and whose lines and spaces dissect the supine female body, thus allowing the artist to reproduce her in detail and perspective. By appropriating the camera, the mechanism for reproduction, Cindy Sherman occupies the privileged position of Dürer's artist and is at the same time the objectified model. Indeed, in one of her photographs, Sherman mimics the reclining pose of Dürer's nude which she could only have captured by defining her gaze at herself along the line of sight first used by Dürer's artist.

Sherman's art, like women working at the nautilus, is the most appropriate image for the era after the struggle to appropriate male-dominated production has been won and then summarily been reabsorbed by capitalism. Not unlike industrial machinery, the machine for photographic production, the camera, was originally associated with great *male* artists: Cartier-Bresson, Stieglitz, Hine. The influx of women photographers in an art world previously dominated by men is fundamentally related to the development of photography as a leisure-time commodity. Only after the camera was domesticated largely by Eastman Kodak to tap the tremendous profitability of home photography did it become accessible to women and children, female photographers and housewives alike.

If the Luddites urged breaking the machinery of capitalism, and Rosie the Riveter represented a temporary feminist usurpation of the machine, then Cindy Sherman, the nautilus of photography, defines intimate oneness with the machine and assimilation into the production process. In the nineteenth century, Marx wrote against the worker's alienation. He demonstrated that in selling labor power, the worker was separated both from control over production and from the fruits of labor, the commodities and profits from their sale. The contradiction of the commodity is that it can be absolutely divorced from the worker while at the same time it is the container of the worker's alienated labor. Alienation informs the entire circuit of production and consumption under capitalism. In such a system, the utopian impulse often finds expression in the very forms that simultaneously articulate its containment. The image of a woman producing herself on the nautilus machine and Cindy Sherman dramatically posing into her self-activated camera are both expressions of women's deep desire to deny alienation. Both articulate the desire to seize control over production and the commodity. Both demonstrate the utopian desire to be in control, to activate the machine. And they express the highly reified desire to be absorbed into the machine's function. Both express the utopian longing to no longer see one's alienated labor in the commodity, but do so by the dystopian formula of making the self into the commodity.

The liberatory impulses are in every instance contained within the larger capitalist system which gives the lie to the notion of feminized production. Cindy Sherman and the nautilus are epiphenomenal metaphors for an era in which more and more women are being brought into the workforce. Many now derive from the middle strata, whose women in the past would have been frozen in the domestic sphere. This means that whatever notions of alterity that previously informed the bourgeois family and home as separate from production

77

are now collapsed as the home, office, and highway merge into every woman's production/reproduction circuit. Then, too, because most women are brought into production as part-time or service workers, their wage labor is as devalued as their domestic labor was (and is) invisible. Images of women at one with the machine, collapsed into a system in which production is simultaneous with reproduction are not alternatives, but rather sublime metaphors for the working woman's place in commodity capitalism.

JEM AND THE HOLOGRAMS

"The simulacrum is the truth": this is Jean Baudrillard's brilliantly succinct way of summarizing all the phenomena of late capitalism, including the receding significance of the referent, the loss of the subject, and the endless flow of mass-produced and fetishized commodities (Baudrillard, 1981). By affirming "the simulacrum" as "the truth," Baudrillard metaphorizes the relationship between production and consumption in late capitalism. Indeed, there is a popular new doll marketed for young girls whose name is Jem and who is a simulacrum, not in the old sense of the term, as every doll is a mimetic representation of a real child or baby, but a simulacrum totally divorced from any possible referent whose only truth is itself. Physically, Jem is a Barbie look-alike: long, thin legs and torso; accentuated breasts; hard, stiff body (made not for play or cuddling, but for posing in her myriad fashions); blue eyes; and synthetic blonde hair. Unlike Barbie, whose media appearances are limited to TV commercials for Barbie, Jem is the star of a weekly cartoon series and her own two-hour video, as well as being a toy marketed from coast to coast. "Record Company executive by day, rock star by night," is the advertising hype for Jem. Actually, Jem's transformations are more frequent than the Wolfman's. This is because she does not require the moon in order to change, but regularly flip-flops between rock star and executive at least three or four times a day. Jem's dual personality brings together all the cultural connotations associated with transformation and identity. She is the schizoid personality, she is also Cinderella, she is the simulacrum who produces her own referent (who, as it turns out, is also a simulacrum), and she is also a very good example of the nautilus/Cindy Sherman syndrome: the woman inside the circuit of production and consumption.

The story of Jem is a little complicated, but most 6-year-old girls can give a fair account of how Jem and her alter ego came about. The greatest difficulty for the child narrator is in attempting to tell which personality is real and why. The story begins with Jerrica, whose mother is long dead and whose father has just died, leaving his daughter heir to the Starlight Record Company, which he owned, and the orphanage, which he acquired as a tax shelter. As executrix and philanthropist, Jerrica quickly runs head on into opposition: the unscrupulous Eric Raymond, who is executor of her father's will and Jerrica's official guardian. Raymond's aim is to take over the record company, thus leaving Jerrica penniless and unable to keep the orphanage going.

However, all is not lost because Jerrica's father has left her another bequest, a marvel of high technology: "a complete music synthesizer and holographic machine!" Cynergy is the machine's name. Endowed with a feminine voice, personality, and face that appears on her video-screen matrix, the machine is Jerrica's fairy godmother. This is where the story becomes difficult to tell for the child, who is most likely to base her narrative on the story of Cinderella. In both the Grimm and the Disney versions of the fairy tale, Cinderella's transformation is enacted at the level of appearance. As the brothers Grimm tell it, Cinderella chants over her mother's grave and a little bird throws down a gold and silver dress and slippers. In Disney's animation, Cinderella cries over her mother's grave and her fairy godmother (an early form of surrogate motherhood) transforms a pumpkin into a coach, mice into horses, and Cinderella's ragged dress into a bouffant ball-gown. Transformations such as these do not pose a problem for the child narrator whose experience of stories is apt to include all the traditional forms, particularly those, like fairy tales, that involve magical explanations. After all, Cinderella, notwithstanding her fancy dress, is still Cinderella.

However, Jerrica's transformation to Jem is another matter altogether, because she really becomes someone else. And if that were not enough, the high-tech holographic machine thoroughly erases all but the most residual traces of those factors that in the Cinderella story function as a reality principle (like the pumpkin and Cinderella's grimy face). Cynergy does not just dress Jerrica up in new attire and give her an acoustic guitar, she produces Jem as a holographic image, who completely replaces her referent, Jerrica. What is more, the machine can also make a holographic image of Jerrica. This means that once the process begins, Jem and Jerrica are simultaneously defined as simulacra and as real. "The simulacrum is the truth."

While watching the Jem video with my 8-year-old daughter, I found myself struggling to define what was real and what was not. In one scene, Jem is about to be run over by a speeding car. "Is that Jem a projection from the machine, or is she really there," I asked. "She's really there," said Stacy, "but Jerrica, when she was standing by the side of the road, was a projection . . . that time." Of course, the whole thing – Jem, Jerrica, their respective projections, the fairy godmother machine – are all animations, which, if we recall the relationship of animation to the film industry, represents something of a technological simulacrum with respect to the cinematic reality of film. What is more, these particular animations are all computer-produced, making them the synthetic antitheses of the original hand-drawn, hand-painted, and hand-inked animations produced by the Disney Studio in the thirties.

The production of art is at stake in the creation of Jem just as it is for Cindy Sherman. This Cinderella is a world-famous musician and lead singer accompanied by the female rock group, the Holograms. Composed of former orphans from Jerrica's home for the homeless, the Holograms have similarly been transformed by the holographic machine. Jem and the Holograms travel around the world cutting gold records, playing to sell-out concerts, and winning every rock music competition they enter. Throughout, they are doggedly pursued by a rival female rock band, the Misfits. This gang of rowdy, evil-doers loses all its music competitions to Jem, and consequently tries to sabotage Jem and her success. What is interesting about the Misfits is that the loud and clearly bad music they play is real. It is their own music, played by themselves on their instruments. Whereas Jem's music, which wins all the prizes and sounds good, is no less a simulacrum than Jem herself. As one of the orphans exclaims when they all first discover Cynergy, "Wow, this is a complete music synthesizer!" From its composition, through realization, to sales, Jem's music, her art, is a product of the machine. This is where Jem as artist and producer rejoins Cindy Sherman and the nautilus machine. Jem is inside the producing machine, playing at being producer and object consumed. She produces her art, and she and her art are produced.

Jem allows us to grasp a larger picture of production not available to us when we focus more narrowly on Cinday Sherman and recognize in her work the positive aspects of a woman artist's appropriation of a field previously defined by men. What we see with Jem is the feminization of production. Cynergy is the machine as woman. She is a surrogate mother for whom there is no difference between creation and procreation. Cynergy offers the young child born into an era when women's rights to economic and social equality are supposed to have been won, the appearance of a production system defined by women and run by women. This, however, is an illusion more false than any simulacraful truth. The absent father who made the machine, bequeathed it to his daughter, and probably controls her through it from the grave, defines the bottom line in capitalist production. The invisible fatherly mastermind suggests a new way of looking at Cynergy – as father surrogate in drag.

FROM FAIRY TALE TO ROMANCE

As storytellers, young girls will find enough similarities between Jem and Cinderella to structure a tale along the lines of the traditional fairy tale. Besides the fairy godmother, and the new rock star dresses, there is also a pair of sparkling rose-colored earrings, Jem's equivalent of the Cinderella slippers. These stay with her from one transformation to the next and function as a magical, techno-cybernetic hook-up with Cynergy. Whenever Jerrica finds herself in trouble, she puts her finger to her earring and chants, "Show time, Cynergy." Immediately, she becomes Jem, who solves the problem and closes the episode by reversing the chant, "Show's over, Cynergy," and Jem becomes Jerrica again.

As they form an audience, young girls who watch Jem on TV function not as tellers, but as readers. From this perspective they are put in a position in which they are instructed on how to read a different popular form, one that will shape their lives as adults to a much greater extent than the fairy tale. This is the romance. For every Cinderella component Jem includes an equally significant narrative feature derived from Harlequin romances. In bringing together the two traditions, Jem extinguishes the contradictions that are more apparent in the older tales by assimilating them to the romance, where contradiction is more thoroughly managed. Grimm's version of Cinderella is a tension-wrought text. In the relationship between Cinderella and her dead mother, the tale demonstrates the potential for strong, nurturing bonding between women, whose antithesis is the equally strong dissension and rivalry between Cinderella and her stepmother. The fairy tale allows young girls fully to experience both sides of women's contradictory relationships and to realize that the way women are – either caring or competitive – is largely determined by their relationship to absent or superficially defined male figures. The deepest contradiction of the fairy tale is the strength of male domination which need not be described in full in order for the Prince to be the solution to Cinderella and the resolution of the tale.

Tania Modleski has written an important essay on the Harlequin romance. Whereas these novels have long been felt to be little more than trashy reading for self-indulgent women, Modleski shows that the romance articulates women's deepest hostilities towards men as well as their own ill-defined longings for autonomy. The romance is, then, the form for the containment of women's aspirations and for the management of social contradiction. Inferring from the texts and their portrayal of women, Modleski concludes on an optimistic note focused on the untapped strength of women's desire: "the fact that the novels must go to such extremes to neutralize women's anger and to make masculine hostility bearable testifies to the depths of women's discontent" (Modleski, 1982: 58).

Jem goes to such extremes to manage the young girl's awareness of the contradictions embedded in the allusion to Cinderella and which are likely to become freshly activated at a time when young girls expect to fulfill all their aspirations and have not yet learned that, while times have changed, the structures of domination that contained their grandmothers continue to the present and may well contain them. Jem's machine-generated talent, success, and body allow her to experience the fruits of her aspirations without ever having to confront the social opposition that any other young girl would have to deal with in order to become a corporate executive, successful musician, and beautiful, many-costumed star. However, the most potent device for the management of contradiction in Jem is the erasure of all adult women figures and the subsequent function of men as the young girl's only socializing influence. The young girl's total dependence (both economic and emotional) on a dominant male figure (whether he be cast as benign or sinister) without recourse to a counterbalancing female character is a fundamental feature of romance. Besides the father and his holographic machine, Jem is conditioned by her relationship to her boyfriend, Rio, a sort of ineffectual Prince Charming; and her combative relationship to Eric Raymond, a stock Harlequin name and character who is as evil as he is handsome. In usurping the young heroine's rightful place as head of Starlight Music, Raymond forms a direct link with the father and demonstrates that while men may pay lip-service to women's equality, real power is still in the hands of men, who may appear to be antagonistic (the one good, the other evil), but are in fact co-conspirators. In developing a comparison between Harlequin romances in North America and the Latin American photonovels and *libros semanales*, Jean Franco coined a succinct pun for the way in which Anglo women are managed and brought into control by the male-dominated network. As she put it, they are "incorporated" (Franco, 1986: 119). This is definitely the case for Jem as it is for many of the Harlequin heroines who strive for careers only to find themselves brought into the corporation as mascots, play pretties, dependent nieces, and finally wives.

Jem's "incorporation" extends into her love relationships, negating the possibility of developing and experiencing her sexuality. In her life and identity as Jerrica, she is defined as girlfriend to Rio, her age-mate and buddy, who helps out at the orphanage and in the daily concerns of rock music administration. They are like old-fashioned high-school "steadies," whose relationship will never become sexual simply because Jerrica is always vanishing, usually at a moment that would have brought her closer to Rio, in order to become Jem. Jem, of course, is extremely attractive and usually in some dire situation, requiring Rio to come to her rescue. Hence, Jem is constantly seducing Rio, who undergoes deep torment over his emotional infidelity to Jerrica. However, the relationship between Jem and Rio will also never be sexual because as soon as the escapade ends, "Show's over" and Jem becomes Jerrica. On the surface this all looks like a complicated way to keep sex out of children's Saturday morning cartoons. Read more deeply and from a liberal perspective, we might be tempted to say that cutting off the development of both love relationships helps teach young girls not to see themselves as wholly defined by a man, love, and marriage. However, read more profoundly and in the context of the way in which patriarchal power dominates the corporation and works through the machine, Jem's inability to continue either her "steady" relationship or her seductive relationship can only be interpreted as an abrupt negation of her adult sexuality. The machine that controls her passage from one identity to another has her perpetually locked at the level of pubescent child. Allowed to establish budding relationships with another man, she is finally and foremost her father's daughter.

Jem as a contemporary women's allegory is a horrific tale. In it, the desire for selfhood is met with a machine-produced body and machine-produced art, while the desire for autonomy is solved by

Photo: Karen Klugman

"incorporation" into the corporation. This is patriarchy nautilus-style. It allows women the false gratification of seeing themselves in the self-made products they constitute. However, because real power lies elsewhere in the larger corporate structure, Jem activates the holograph and is the hologram, just as you or I, when we activate the nautilus and become its finely honed body, enact the expropriation of ourselves as producers and the alienation of ourselves as consumers.

BACKGROUND SOURCES AND
FURTHER READING

In their depictions of women's bodies (whether these be directly representational or more metaphoric and symbolic), women artists and intellectuals use their work (whether it be descriptive or analytical) to engage with the sexual and political, the personal and public, the organic and technological.

Haraway, Donna (1987) "A manifesto for Cyborgs," *Australian Feminist Studies* 4.

Haug, Frigga (1987) *Female Sexualization: A Collective Work of Memory*, London: Verso.

Irigaray, Luce (1985a) *Speculum of the Other Woman*, Ithaca: Cornell University Press.

——(1985b) *This Sex Which Is Not One*, Ithaca: Cornell University Press.

Kahlo, Frida, paintings, especially the self-portraits.

Kuhn, Annette (1988) "The body and cinema: some problems for feminism," in Susan Sheridan (ed.), *Grafts*, London: Verso.

Morrison, Toni (1987) *Beloved*, New York: Alfred A. Knopf.

O'Keefe, Georgia, paintings, particularly *One Hundred Flowers*.

Williamson, Judith (1986) "It's different for girls," in *Consuming Passions*, London: Marion Boyars.

5

PLAYING HOUSE
Domestic labor as culture

"You be baby, I be mommy"

Charlotte, age 2

When a housewife takes her family's clothes off the line or out of the dryer, sorts them, and leaves them in neat little piles for the rest of the family members to put away, she performs one of the repetitive daily tasks that defines domestic labor as the creation of use value. The distinction between the home as the site for the creation of use value and the workplace where exchange values are produced is one of the points Sally Alexander developed in her study of women's work in the nineteenth century. As she put it, capitalism intervened into a pre-existing sexual division of labor to exacerbate the subordination of homeplace and wife:

> By distinguishing between production for use and production for exchange, and by progressively subordinating the former to the latter, by confining production of use to the private world of the home and female labor, and production for exchange increasingly to the workshop outside the home, and male labor, capitalism ensured the economic dependence of women upon their husbands or fathers for a substantial part of their lives.
>
> (Alexander, 1976: 77)

Today a housewife's labor is very rarely seen as productive. She seldom actually makes her family's clothes; rather, she daily replenishes their use. As with the maintenance of clothing, all the tasks performed in the home ensure that those family members who work outside the home for pay will go out of the door in the morning capable of making commodities for exchange; and hence, actively contributing to the creation of surplus value. This is the economics of production under capitalism. Currently, there is some debate as to whether

86

or not work performed by women in the home contributes to the production of surplus value. It might be argued that women's labor in the home produces a value-creating commodity: labor power. Or it might be said that the housewife indirectly enhances her husband's time spent producing surplus value. The Women's Studies Group at the University of Birmingham, states its position this way: domestic labor as "the production of use values under non-wage relations of production, within the capitalist mode of production [does not] contribute directly to the creation of surplus value" (Women's Studies Group, 1978).

As I see it, no matter how we construe the economics of domestic labor, our culture as a lived experience defines a dramatic split between home and workplace. This separation is so much a part of the ideology of late twentieth-century capitalism that the piece-work produced by many women in their homes (including after-hours typing and garment assembly) is as invisible as domestic labor itself. Such labor does not disrupt the notion of the home as a privatized world. The housewife's labor and the use value she creates are culturally perceived as "outside" the labor process and are, therefore, rendered all but invisible. All those neat little piles of clothes stacked end to end could stretch from Maine to California and still the society as a whole would not see in them the production of use. Indeed, women artists have mounted exhibitions that highlight the repetitive nature of the work of reproducing daily life. One such is a series of photographs assembled by the southern California artist Elenore Antin. These show great quantities of boots and shoes that Antin put in long lines and photographed in such a way as to show the shoes rounding corners, disappearing over hills, or entering buildings. Where women on welfare are apt to interpret the lines of shoes as representing the experience of waiting on line for social services, women in the middle classes are more apt to interpret the shoe series as an expression of commodity seriality and the repetitious nature of daily tasks.

Much recent attention has focused on gender roles. Certainly the number of major research projects funded by the Rockefeller Foundation has stimulated inquiry into how gender is related to the socially ascribed roles for men and women. In terms of domestic labor, the common line of reasoning has been to denounce the polarization of gender roles in the home and urge that men assume responsibility for many household tasks as a way of combating male domination. So, then, what if the woman's husband did all the washing, drying, and

Photo: Karen Klugman

sorting of the family clothes? Would this change the nature of the work? Or even the way in which it is perceived? Marxist feminists generally maintain that patriarchy pre-dates capitalism and that capitalist economic structures have simply incorporated male domination into them. Following this line of argument, we might say that men's performance of household labor undermines patriarchal notions about gender, but it does not affect the economic subordination of domestic labor to wage labor.

A different approach to women's oppression in the home is to focus on the privatization of domestic work and the isolation of the housewife. In simple and grim terms, the housewife is "Isolated, the only adult in a private house" (Women's Studies Group, 1978: 36). Yet, she is the only one who will meet her children's needs and demands. Both Janice Radway (1984) and Tania Modleski (1982), in their studies of women's popular fiction, point to the oppressive nature of living solely for another's needs in their explanations of why women "escape" into romance. Isolated, but not alone; giving care, but never replenished, the woman experiences the home as a prison house which is both physically and emotionally draining. Within this characterization of domestic labor, one corrective strategy might be to recreate the extended family and to apportion household chores more evenly between all household members. So, then, what if the woman's children performed all the tasks required to maintain the family's clothes? Would this render use value socially appreciable?

I would argue that only the failure to create use value can be made visible. Say the housewife left all the clothes in the dryer for a week – just let them pile up until nobody had anything to wear. The absence of replenished use value would be remarked upon, whereas its creation is simply taken for granted.

Why is this so? The answer is that what counts in capitalism is exchange value. This is a wage labor society. If you do not work for a wage, you are not felt to be a worker. This is a commodified society. If your activities do not include making, selling, or buying commodities, your endeavors are not seen as making a contribution. The question I will pose from a number of perspectives throughout this chapter is how we might begin to restore the importance of use value in a society where everything is measured against exchange. What is more, I want to ask if we can imagine use value itself as something that is not already overshadowed by its relationship to exchange value. Even as we recognize that housework constitutes the creation of use values, we must not assume that our experience of use value under capitalism is any less fetishized than our experience of commodities. We tend to associate commodity fetishism only with the production of exchange

values. In contrast, use value is felt to be pure and autonomous, something that harks back to precapitalist societies where use and the circulation of useful objects was a cementing bond between people. This notion of use value does not pertain today. Those piles of laundered clothes awaiting the children who will put them away in drawers and closets are little different from the cans of peas on the supermarket shelf. Both exemplify the erasure of the labor and social relations that go into their production. It is striking how commodity capitalism, then, finds ways to re-introduce the presence of lost labor. For instance, there is now a new line of products marketed to render use value perceptible. These are the "fresh scents" and static-free sheets that the housewife can buy in order to put appreciable traces of her care and labor into her laundry. This is a commodity culture's response to the absolute impossibility of demonstrating the social nature of use value. Can we confront the tremendous influence of the commodity form in our daily lives by struggling to recognize the social value of use in domestic labor? Can we imagine what the piles of clothes would look like to a society that had not invented the commodity form? Such a stretch of the imagination may well be possible only in feminist science fiction. Short of exercising the imagination to such an extent, and in the real world of opposition politics, some Marxist feminists have promoted wages for housework as a means of eliminating women's oppression: "Pay women – not the military" (Brown, 1983: 23). This would be tantamount to changing the larger economy. If women are subordinated because domestic labor is invisible, then wages for housework creates parity with labor done outside the home for pay. Selma James advances the argument to suggest that wages for housework would also amend women's inferior position in workplace jobs: "The subordination to the wage of the man in the home and the subordinating nature of [domestic] labor weakens the woman wherever else she is working" (James, 1975: 18). Wages for housework represents the most highly developed position one can take while in a capitalist economy and struggling toward a Marxian economy. It is guided by the cold, hard line of economic reasoning. It fully abandons the possibility of redeeming the social significance of use value and affirms exchange value as the basis for struggle and the measure for all value.

These are some of the issues generated by the extensive work being done by feminists (primarily Marxist and socialist) to define the economics of domestic labor. This chapter is not aimed at resolving any of the economic debates or breaking any of the loggerheads that emerge in the process of working through the relationship of patriarchy to capitalism and wage labor to domestic labor. Rather, my aim is to explore an entirely new dimension: domestic labor as it is defined and experienced culturally. Work along these lines intersects with the economic and may well provide a means of gaining a fresh perspective on domestic labor under capitalism. I do not want to suggest that developing radical positions in culture will in itself change the economics of domestic labor, but I do maintain that revolutionary perspectives on culture can transform the way in which we approach and define economic issues.

PEEK-A-BOO: THE INVISIBLE BECOMES VISIBLE

When working in the area of cultural analysis, we need to remind ourselves that everything is historical. Because culture is so taken for granted, so much a part of daily life, so like a second skin, we have a tendency to regard it as transhistorical. The challenge to critics of culture is to remember that the cultural practices and artifacts that are typical today may well have been atypical for our parents and may not even have existed for our grandparents. This has important consequences for the study of domestic labor. One of the things that most interests me is when and how domestic labor becomes visible in the first place so as to be defined as an object for study. While the actual work of reproducing the labor force has been a constant historical necessity to capitalism, the notion of domestic labor as an economic category becomes visible only at certain times and under certain conditions.

In assessing the work of the post-sixties Women's Movement, the Women's Studies Group at the University of Birmingham, found that: "The early writings of the current . . . women's movement . . . concentrated on the articulation of the experience of housework. The concern was primarily to bring to *visibility* women's work in the home, and to have it recognized as work" (Women's Studies Group, 1978: 36). Because we are living at a time when domestic labor and gender roles are hot issues for feminists and the media alike, we may not be aware of how little attention was paid to domestic labor in the past. Domestic labor clearly became an issue in the twentieth century. Besides the post-sixties, there were two other periods when domestic labor emerged as a visible social phenomenon. One of these was during the Depression, when social and economic upheaval sundered peoples' relationships to jobs and to the way they conceived jobs, productivity, needs, and social roles. During this period, two women were at the forefront of inquiry into domestic labor: Grace Hutchins and Mary Inman. Both developed resounding critiques of women's work under capitalism. Inman laid the groundwork for reckoning the value of women's domestic labor with respect to the maintenance of the labor force (Inman, 1987: 308), while Hutchins is most noted for condemning the "double burden" of working-class women, who work for wages and return home to the demands of husband and family (Hutchins, 1987: 335).

The other historical period when women's domestic labor emerged out of the otherwise smothering broadcloth of the American industrial economy was the decade following the Second World War. This was a time when many women, who had left domestic life to take wartime factory jobs, found themselves obliged by husbands and employers to return to the domestic labor force, thus making it possible for men to resume their places in the industrial economy. As many social and cultural commentators have shown, the fifties was a time of readjustment to domestic life, made possible and palatable by the postwar development of consumer goods, including new home-care appliances and new home media entertainments.

I want to suggest, then, as a working hypothesis, that the 1930s, 1950s and post-1960s, are the periods when domestic labor erupted into social visibility. If we take these as the high-water marks of social ferment, we must also be aware that the way we perceive these periods is greatly influenced by the history of domestic technology that has provided each generation in the twentieth century with its own array of appliances and gadgets. Our efforts to extend an understanding of domestic labor into cultural dimensions will of necessity involve an archaeology of material culture, whose most fascinating and most understudied sector comprises children's toys. The technology of each era is replicated in its toys. Women who are mothers today may have played with toy brooms, dustpans, irons, and ironing boards when they were children, but will not find these toys widely marketed in the eighties. Instead the mass-produced and widely sold toy that best defines domestic labor today is a child-size, red and yellow, plastic shopping basket. Cheap in price and only slightly more popular with girls than boys, the toy shopping basket testifies to the extent that domestic labor has merged with the supermarket and commodity consumption.

Something more is at stake than a simple correspondence between toys and technology. Indeed, certain toys truly punctuate those moments when domestic labor becomes visible in much the same way that post-sixties feminist theory also marks such a moment. For instance, the doll's house is a concrete metaphor for the coming into being and development of the bourgeois class. Like the mercantile bourgeoisie that it replicates, the doll's house originated in Amsterdam in the seventeenth century. Unlike the later doll's houses that followed the bourgeoisie to France and England, the early Dutch doll's houses were equally organized around working and living spaces. One of the first doll's houses, owned by Petronella Dunois in the late seventeenth century and now on display in the Rijksmuseum, Amsterdam, includes an upper floor given over to a laundry and a nursery and a lower floor comprising a large kitchen and pantry. Only the middle floor, consisting of two rooms, might be called the family's living space, having no recognizable work built into the decor (Glubok, 1984).

This was not the case by the nineteenth century, when the doll's house exemplified the consolidation of the bourgeois class and with it the extensive erasure of domestic labor. In British doll's houses of the Victorian period, fully 90 percent of the household space is allotted the family's living and leisure-time space whereas the kitchen and maids' quarters are little niches. A survey of European doll's houses reveals the progressive erasure of domestic labor century by century, corresponding to the development of the bourgeoisie. The doll's house is the preeminent expression of the origin of the nuclear family and the private world of the home. What is more, doll's houses represent a very important phenomenological dimension: that is, the translation of social activities into the objects that represent those activities, and the translation of social relationships into spatial relationships. Such objectification is itself coincidental with capitalism. It demonstrates the penetration of the commodity form into daily life that was first and most profoundly felt by the class that could afford commodity consumption on a broad scale: the bourgeoisie.

COOKING WITH ANNIE, BETTY, AND BARBIE

Coinciding with the 1930s, 1950s, and post-1960s, as moments when domestic labor became visible, there is a particular children's toy whose design and mode of use can tell us a lot about domestic labor in each of those periods. The toy is a play cooking stove. While miniature ranges evolved with doll's house furnishings, free-standing metal units that a child might play with on the floor or mounted on a shelf or counter-top did not come into existence until the era after the First World War. One such model, marketed in 1933, included three oven doors and a surface range. Done up in "Depression green," the stove was made more festive with numerous images of Orphan Annie and her dog, Sandy. In relation to the history of domestic technology, the Orphan Annie stove marks the great expansion in gas and electric appliances for household use throughout the twenties and thirties, particularly in urban areas.

There are two observations I would make about the Orphan Annie toy stove that have important implications for domestic labor as a cultural experience. First of all, this is an early example of a media spin-off toy. I want to emphasize this point because it relates to a basic tenet developed by Marxist feminists that understands the household as the primary site of commodity consumption. The household may be outside the circuit of production, but it is crucial to the growth of the capitalist economy. To this I would add that consumption and the household are embraced by the media. Consumers today would be shocked to find a significant number of commodities that were *not* media spin-offs. Almost everything we buy our children, from the original Mickey Mouse watches, to Lion-O bed sheets, to Ghostbusters lunch-boxes, and Flintstones vitamins, is an emblematic representation of the media. This was only beginning to be the case in the 1930s. The little girl whose parents bought her the Orphan Annie stove for Christmas in 1933 had the unique possibility of uniting her world of play with the media fantasy world of Little Orphan Annie. Children today assume that their toys and school supplies will be stamped with logo-like references to TV cartoon series. What would be remarkable in today's mass toy market would be the absence of cartoon figures.

The other cultural factor that the Orphan Annie stove documents is the freeing of some young girls (in families who could afford to buy the stove) from appreciable amounts of real domestic labor. I say this because in order to conceptualize cooking, or any other productive activity, as play, one must have the free time to do so and also recognize the distinction between the real performance (and performers) of such activities, and their playful counterparts. The young girl who was freed from real cooking tasks to play with her Orphan Annie stove was, however, not freed into an independent world of play, but rather reabsorbed into the family by way of the domestic nature of the play. I want to make an important distinction between play that is organized around a toy like the Orphan Annie stove and spontaneous forms of play that are not centered on a commodity. For as long as dolls have existed, children (predominantly little girls) have played house and acted out all the caring activities that looking after a baby entails. Play cooking is certainly one of these. What I am remarking in the existence of the play stove is the manifest separation between real cooking and pretend cooking, and at the same time the organization of the play so that it replicates the way real cooking is done, presumably by adults. This is a particular institutionalized form of play. It is very different from the way young children throw leaves, sticks, sand, and water into a bowl or pot, stir it up, and say that they have "cooked" a stew. Play cooking organized around the Orphan Annie stove represents a young girl's separation from the daily performance of household tasks like cooking, while at the same time it ensures that she is "placed on hold"; that is, she will have enough of an idea of what real cooking entails so that when she is an adult with her own appliance-filled kitchen she will see the gas range as a larger version of her childhood plaything.

Unlike some ten or so years ago, many adolescents from the middle classes now cook for themselves and their families. They make frozen TV dinners and Ragu sauce-from-a-jar spaghetti, or they call out for

pizza. These are the children of "two-income families," whose mothers and fathers return home at 6:00 p.m. or later, stressed out and with no idea what to cook for dinner. Some social commentators writing in newspapers have begun to make comparisons between these more affluent children, who cook by default, and the children of working-class parents, who in past decades have worked either with their mothers or by themselves to prepare evening meals from basic foodstuffs. The situations are not at all analogous. What I find significant is that for a number of decades many children from the middle classes were excluded from the performance of actual domestic labor. Now some are assuming the work of maintaining a household, but under the new and very different situation of readily available commodities. Some feminists, particularly in Britain, have pointed to recent trends in fast-food consumption as evidence of the "socialization" of domestic labor (Women's Studies Group, 1978: 44). This is seen as a positive development. The argument is that as more and more women work outside the home for pay, the role of the housewife simply disappears and the family's needs are met in the consumption of goods produced outside the home in the society at large. This line of reasoning poses problems for us in the United States. To point to the "socialization" of domestic labor in Britain where some forms of socialized services exist, may well give rise to images of what a fuller socialist economics might be like, in which domestic needs would be met in larger living and working social units. The British reader might be led to imagine communal cooking and eating halls where families might congregate after school and work. In contrast, a reader in the United States who encounters the notion of the "socialization" of domestic labor, and has only capitalist economics to draw on, is apt to envision the quick commodity fix at the local Burger King as society's way of de-privatizing housework. By its very nature, commodity consumption is at odds with community and cannot promote the "socialization" of domestic labor, but rather its individualization. Everyone may be able to afford the cheapest hamburger at McDonald's, but this does not mean that domestic labor in the United States is in any danger of becoming "socialized."

In the 1950s parents could buy their little girls the Betty Crocker E-Z Bake Oven. Twice the size of the Orphan Annie stove and done in shiny white, it resembled a proper 1950s kitchen unit. In fact, it really worked. Equipped with a light bulb in the rear, the oven could heat sufficiently to bake a small pre-packaged Betty Crocker cake-mix cake. Here the media tie-in is to the persona of modern housewifery:

Betty Crocker herself, whose cheery face could be seen in daytime TV commercials as well as on the supermarket shelves. From our vantage-point in the early 1990s world of Madonna and Whitney Houston, we may find it inconceivable that a lively young girl in the 1950s might have ever considered modeling herself after Betty Crocker. Yet efficient housewifery was the ideological counterpoint to

By permission of Mattel UK Ltd

an era under the spell of modernization and progress. Indeed, there is a Barbie doll from the early sixties whose outfit includes a checkered apron, a wooden spoon, and dramatically spiked high heels. She is certainly the embodiment of domestic glamour.

What I find most interesting in the E-Z Bake Oven is the need to reintroduce actual production in a play cooking situation. If the Orphan Annie stove represents the separation between play and work, the Betty Crocker E-Z Bake Oven reproduces real work, but belittles it by scaling down the cake to child size. Domestic labor is indeed child's play.

The need to make play cooking real oddly collides with an era when modernization meant an influx of pre-assembled, pre-measured, prepared, and packaged foods like the cake from a mix. These eliminated much of the labor time spent on domestic chores and expanded the time devoted to domestic shopping. Prepared foods also demonstrate the corporate annexation of the household. In the world of the late 1950s the E-Z Bake Oven taught the child that what is real (that is, what you know is real because you really make it) is the commodity. This is an important moment in the history of our relationship to the commodity form. It stands at a midway point between a society's remembrance of what it must have been like to produce a lot of useful objects from scratch and the recognition that in the future the commodity form will be the substance of daily life. In associating the real with the commodity the E-Z Bake Oven demonstrates another important feature of the commodity form: it is special. Commodities may be the substance of mundane daily life, but they present themselves as unique; and, like cakes, fit for a celebration. The commodity promises that every event will be a festival. Real cooking is cooking junk food.

The 1980s equivalent of the Orphan Annie and E-Z Bake Oven is the Fisher-Price kitchen unit, an entire one-quarter size, interconnected kitchen featuring oven, range, refrigerator, sink, cupboards, and drawers. For its extremely compact dimensions considering the vast number of features and functions it offers, the Fisher-Price unit resembles up-to-date kitchen engineering condominium-style. Unlike the two previous stoves, which merely replicated the colors of the appliances ordinarily found in the kitchens of those eras, the Fisher-Price unit is done up in the bold primary colors – red, yellow, and blue – that are synonymous with the company's entire line of toys. In children's toys, color has been a logo ever since Tonka first made yellow trucks.

As its mixed-gender advertising demonstrates, the Fisher-Price unit is definitely a kitchen for the 1980s. Many progressive day-care centers that organize play around particular areas, designated as dress-up area, block area, and story area, are choosing the Fisher-Price unit for their kitchen play areas. Similarly, many parents regularly shop for Fisher-Price toys and are choosing to buy the kitchen unit for their daughters and their sons. And why not? Many more fathers are cooking today than in past generations.

The parent who buys his or her child a Fisher-Price kitchen immediately discovers the need to buy all the fascinating accessories that go with it (but are not included in the original package). Apart from doll's houses, which would be nothing without the continuous acquisition of furnishings and family members, model railroads are the only other example of an early mass-produced toy that was marketed on the concept of continued consumption within the same series. Once a parent bought the locomotive and train, the track bed and power box, he or she then had to acquire one by one all those moving and flashing signal lights and animated buildings. A more contemporary example is Barbie. Having a Barbie doll means very little in itself without a full wardrobe of Barbie's fashions. Today, almost every toy on the mass market requires continued consumption in the same series. The Fisher-Price unit necessitates an incredible array of foods and utensils, all simulated in plastic. There are plastic waffles that pop into the plastic toaster. There are plastic french fries and hamburgers, not to mention plastic eggs that when cracked open reveal a simulated scrambled yolk. There are also numerous ancillary appliances, such as the battery-operated saucepan that is filled with plastic confetti held in liquid suspension so that it appears to bubble and boil when you switch it "on."

In the Fisher-Price kitchen, the differences between the simulacrum and the real is only just distinguishable. If the Betty Crocker E-Z Bake Oven represented a moment at which people began to associate the commodity with the real, then the Fisher-Price unit, marketed at the height of the consumer society, suggests that the difference between a "real" frozen waffle that you "cook" in the toaster and the Fisher-Price plastic version is only a question of calories. Something of the same might be said for the distinction between McDonald's fries and the Fisher-Price fries; and for that between supermarket eggs, which are produced under factory conditions, and the Fisher-Price factory-made eggs.

Earlier, I mentioned that many young boys are encouraged to play with the Fisher-Price kitchen. I want to assess what seems to be a positive change in gender roles in the light of John Fiske's analysis of *Miami Vice* (Fiske, 1987). Fiske points to a "feminization of masculinity" that we might be tempted to apply to the influx of men into the kitchen and the number of young boys learning to appreciate cooking with the Fisher-Price kitchen. In developing his analysis Fiske draws on the commonly accepted fact of capitalist economics that women are primarily defined as consumers. This is a line of reasoning that many feminists have taken up. For instance, in her book on the department store, entitled *Just Looking*, Rachel Bowlby shows how the construction of femininity is very much like shopping. A women is being looked at (consumed by the male gaze) while looking at and consuming commodities for sale. A women's sense of self is of a self being consumed while she is herself consuming (Bowlby, 1985: 32). What Fiske goes on to show is that *Miami Vice* puts its macho masculine figures, Crockett and Tubbs, in the position traditionally defined as feminine. We viewers consume them with our eyes while they are shown to be unabashed consumers of luxury commodities, such as cologne, gold chains, and platinum cigarette cases and lighters. While Fiske applauds *Miami Vice* for the way it feminizes its male heroes, I think we might step back from both the TV program and the Fisher-Price kitchen unit and question whether what is going on is the feminization of masculinity or the commodification of both men and women. It may well be that capitalism, having exploited the women's market, is now reaching out to make men equal to women as consumers. It is true that many more men now participate in shopping as a leisure-time activity (particularly in shopping malls) than would ever have dreamed of doing so in the past. Gender roles are changing, but so too are the economics of commodity capitalism.

LET'S PLAY HOUSE

In chapter 2 I developed the point that when children play they put use value into their commodities: that is, toys. Commodities are the hollowed-out representations of the social relations that go into their production but which are erased under capitalist production. In play, children use their toys to create a context for the recovery of these social relationships. When they play with superhero action figures, little boys decide between themselves what roles they will enact and how they will relate to each other. Good guy, bad guy, sorcerer, or super-brute – the toy figure is a pretext for defining a complicated system of social relationships between the players. Children are not aware of the social relations that are erased in the production of their plastic superhero figures, thus rendering each an example of commodity fetishism; but their play demonstrates that they are truly aware of the social relationships that constitute use. Much of children's play involves discussion and dispute over social relationships.

"You be baby, I be mommy": this is how my own daughter, Charlotte, initiates every game of "house." She does not say, "Let's play house." After all, the house is only the context for the definition of roles. What she is in effect saying is "Let's play role reversal."

The amazing fact about children's domestic role-playing games is that more than 50 percent of the game is spent simply deciding the roles each child will assume. I once observed a group of boys attempting to play a game of "house." They had decided on a father, a couple of brothers, and a son. The game fell apart when they tried to make one of the boys "servant." Clearly, someone had to do the work, and clearly father, brothers, and son had better things to do. With no girls to play mother and no thoughts of gender crossing, the game ended for want of a "servant." (Although it could well have continued if the boys had considered the male technological solution and made one of the family members into a robot.) The process of role debating and role assigning took about half an hour. Although the game never really started, the entire time was devoted to a form of play, as the father, brothers, son, and unassigned others were all in the process of working out their roles and testing their relationships.

In her comprehensive study of the bases for women's oppression, Michele Barrett makes an important distinction between the "ideology of the family" and the "household" (Barrett, 1980). The ideology of the family is the place where patriarchy and capitalism coincide to ensure the oppression of women. Where patriarchy would see women solely as procreators of the species, capitalism inferiorizes women by making social reproduction secondary to the economics of production. The family binds women's nurturing functions to the status of economic marginality. In contrast, I propose that Barrett's notion of household suggests a possible site for imagining social relationships that include family, but transcend its ideology. As Barrett defines it the household is the organizational center for all the material factors that enter into domestic labor. I want to take Barrett's objective conceptualization of household one step further and make it the basis for beginning to think of how we might transform daily-life social relationships. Such a conceptualization of household requires that we actively engage in questioning people's roles and relationships. It is not enough that the patriarch washes the dishes. What the examples drawn from children's play demonstrate is that the roles are of less importance than the process of deciding the roles, and the relationships between people are of less consequence than the efforts made to change the relationships. My intent is not to prioritize childhood, but to suggest that because children in our society have largely been freed from work into play, they are in situations where their efforts are spent experimenting with social relationships, testing the limits, redefining themselves and their friends. When Charlotte begins the game, "You be baby, I be mommy," she puts herself in a situation where she experiments with the complicated combination of authority and nurturing: "Now baby, eat your dinner," "Now baby, don't cry," "Now baby, go to sleep." Do we adults use our households as contexts for actively creating, exploring, reversing social relationships? Or do we spend each day re-enacting gender and role assumptions? Charlotte's play does both.

It recreates all the traditional gender categories; but, by the very nature of play, it sets these at a distance where they become objects to ponder, to subvert or teasingly support, to experience with enjoyment or anger.

The concept of household holds forth extremely important possibilities of reconceptualizing familial relationships – but the forces of patriarchy and capitalism are exceedingly resourceful in their efforts to contain new directions in our thinking about society as well as social change itself. I want to give two examples from contemporary mass culture that demonstrate the containment of all the hopeful possibilities that the conceptualization of household holds forth. The first of these is the TV series *Full House*. This is an extremely interesting exercise in patriarchy 1980s-style. The show features a widowed father of three young girls and the father's two single male room-mates, who, in the show's kinship system, become known as "uncles." *Full House* makes every episode topical. Domestic chores and gender are at issue on a weekly basis: "It's your turn to change the diapers / pack the school lunches / do the shopping." One can see the men sorting and stacking those neat little piles of freshly washed clothes. However, the possibility of overturning male dominance is absolutely denied by the obvious reassertion of patriarchy that puts three adult men in charge of three female children. To be a woman is to be a child; adulthood is manhood. A woman's only operative power is, thus, the old standby: coyness and subversion. "Here, Uncle Jesse, will you remove my stinger?" This is what one of the little girls says as she pokes her bee-costumed butt into her father's room-mate's face. "Uncle" Jesse, of course, rolls his eyes and the show ends with a bit of canned laughter. What is interesting about *Full House* is its wide appeal to children of varying ages. I have observed children from 3 years old to 16, contentedly wrapped up in the TV dilemmas of fatherhood. Everyone knows authority is at stake just as everyone knows authority will not be truly undermined. In the patriarchal approach to toilet training, the "Dads" simply tell the toddler that since she can now walk, she will have to walk to the potty like the rest of them. The show puts men in nurturing positions only to represent authority and redefine patriarchal sexual relationships.

The power of patriarchy to reaffirm itself in situations where men assume the caring roles traditionally ascribed to women has led me to question one of my long-held political convictions. Like many women, I was heartened to see post-1960s work crews composed of men and women: there are women construction workers, town maintenance workers, telephone line "persons." Yet, like many women, I was dismayed by how little challenged gender has been by women's access to many traditional male roles. It occurred to me that the real socially transformative struggle might not be for women to achieve muscle-producing jobs, or even the headships of corporations, but for men to struggle in masses to be nurses, teachers, dieticians, recreation directors, social workers – all the low-paying, socially sustaining jobs that are inevitably associated with women's caring roles in the home and reserved for women in the workforce (Barrett, 1980: 157). *Full House* suggests that in a society where social reproduction is under-valued, men in caregiving roles will not transform the economics of capitalism, but they will provide a means for the reaffirmation of patriarchy.

The other example of how commodity capitalism contains the notion of household and prevents its becoming the site for transforma-tional thinking about gender is apparent in the new *HG* magazine, formally known as the sedate and stuffy *House and Garden*. The magazine's new pages feature intimate peeks into tastefully stunning decor. These are the furnishing, accessories, arrangements, color, fabrics, and the decorators who put them all together to define and promote the new yuppie society. Whatever changes might be happen-ing at large in terms of gender and class (and in terms of the abandonment of the older *House and Garden* clientele in favor of the new *HG* readership) are not at question because the magazine's photo-layout presents the illusion that social relationships are analogous to spatial relationships. The erasure of the social is achieved in a more complete fashion than it was in the nineteenth-century doll's house where one still had a sense of social hierarchy represented in the upstairs, downstairs, and attic arrangements of household tasks and occupants. The new *HG* represents the containment of the potentially transformative notion of household, because everything in it is not shown in dynamic relationship, but is instead presented as a commodity. Everything is photographed, flattened, packaged, and made to look as accessible as the magazine's advertisements for cars, clothes, and cologne. The new *HG* demonstrates how commodity capitalism denies the possibility of depicting social activity and relationships by absorbing active social process into the decorative and spatial.

The change from *House and Garden* to the logo-inspired *HG* summons up a particularly important association with the professional men's fashion magazine, *GQ*. The suggestion is that the transition from the specifically feminine connotations of house and garden to the monogrammatic shorthand of *HG* indicates that many men are now assuming domestic tasks previously deemed fitting only for women. I tend to see the new *HG* in the light of the criticism I brought to bear on previous examples of the "feminization of masculinity." If the new *HG* suggests that the upkeep of domestic and garden space is now an acceptable endeavor for men, it does so under the sign of the logo and in relation to the optimal commodification of horticultural and domestic activities, products, and the settings that these produce.

We may well condemn the way in which male domination has largely confined women to labor in the home and in the garden while excluding many from employment in the workplace. Nevertheless, women in different regions, at different points in time, and in different economic situations have found ways to make their homes and gardens into the visible custodians of their labor. In supplanting the more womanly and out-of-date *House and Garden*, the new *HG* does more than sweep away the privileged middle-class connotations the magazine once had. It effectively buries all past periods when women's work in the house and garden was valued because it was recognized as integral to the wellbeing of the society as a whole. In our enthusiasm for the unisex, uniclass *HG*, we ought not to forget the example of seventeenth-century New England. This was a time when house and garden truly traced the limits of a woman's world. Behind the closed doors and straight wooden house-fronts that typify colonial

New England architecture, women performed their indoor house-keeping tasks. Such labor was largely invisible. But every indoor task had its visible referent in the seventeenth-century dooryard garden. Here in the space between door and street, women cultivated herbs: the sage and comfrey, and countless others needed to preserve and flavor food, cure the sick, dye fabrics, and aromatize household interiors. The dooryard garden was a growing testament to the multiplicity of women's productive roles. They nursed and healed the sick, they clothed and fed their families, they decorated their homes, and they were artists who created in the landscaping code of the time a personal aesthetic out of crushed oyster-shell walkways, raised beds, and plant arrangements.

The seventeenth-century New England dooryard garden poses a challenge to us living in the last decade of the twentieth century. Can we today imagine the productive unit of household and dooryard garden as anything but confining? Can we step back from our centuries' long struggle to expand the terrain of women's labor, not to recreate the seventeenth century, but to grasp how such a productive unit affirmed the social value of women's domestic labor? Can we use the example of the dooryard garden to re-educate ourselves in order to make fresh assessments of domestic labor today? If commodity capitalism turns the products of domestic labor into fetishized objects, the dooryard garden turns living objects into the concrete manifestations of social value.

By focusing on domestic labor from a number of cultural perspectives, we can begin to imagine possible utopian household alternatives that would inhibit the influences of patriarchy and commodity capitalism. Such a project is not new to women's thinking and writing. As Jane Tompkins demonstrates in her astutely political reading of *Uncle Tom's Cabin*, Harriet Beecher Stowe quickened her reader's imagination with a view into a wholly transformed nation that would be centred, not in government or capitalist economics, but in the Quaker settlement kitchen. This is the kitchen of Rachel Halliday, where "the preparation of breakfast exemplifies the way people will work in the ideal society; there will be no competition, no exploitation, no commands" (Tompkins, 1985: 143). In such a world, the elimination of patriarchy could not be more explicit. As Tompkins points out, "Stowe reconceives the role of men in human history: while Negroes, children, mothers, and grandmothers do the world's primary work, men [are portrayed grooming] themselves contentedly in a corner" (Tompkins, 1985: 146).

Similar images of radically transformed domestic space occur throughout contemporary black women's writing. When Toni Morrison takes us as readers into Pilate's house in *Song of Solomon*, she puts us at the center of a communal social space where women participate equally in domestic tasks without the need for authority: where economic independence does not promote a desire for profit; and where a simple task, like boiling an egg, can be infinitely pleasurable. I have argued that the "three-woman households" that occur throughout Morrison's writing enable the author to reconceptualize social and sexual relationships along utopian lines (Willis, 1987b). These involve heterosexual relationships that are not oppressive, and relationships between women across generations that do not obtain in male-dominated nuclear families.

Culture is a battleground, where for centuries the impulse to transform domestic labor – and with it, society as a whole – collides with the containing and oppressive forces of patriarchy and capitalism. The challenge is to recognize utopian moments in culture and use these as a basis for criticizing instances where patriarchy is not condemned, but reasserted; and where social relationships are not redeemed but converted into fetishized objects.

BACKGROUND SOURCES AND FURTHER READING

The following texts provide a basis for making connections between the economics of domestic labor in capitalism, the inferiorization of housework, and women's oppression.

Barrett, Michele (1980) *Women's Oppression Today: Problems in Marxist Feminist Analysis*, London: Verso.
Beechey, Veronica (1987) *Unequal Work*, London: Verso.
Glazer-Malbin, Nona (1979) "Housework: a review essay," *Signs* I: 905–22.
Oakley, Ann (1974) *Women's Work: The Housewife Past and Present*, New York: Pantheon.
Women's Studies Group, Centre for Contemporary Cultural Studies. University of Birmingham (1978) *Women Take Issue*, London: Hutchinson.

Historical developments in the technology of domestic labor can provide a means of understanding the relationship between industrial and domestic labor, and the bearing that this has on gender.

Bose, Christine (1979) "Technology and changes in the division of labor in the American home," *Women's Studies International Quarterly* 2.

Cowan, Ruth Schwartz (1976) "The industrial revolution in the home: household technology and social change in the 20th century," *Technology and Culture* 17: 1–23.

Ewen, Stuart, and Ewen, Elizabeth (1982) *Channels of Desire*, New York: McGraw-Hill.

Gray, Ann (1987) "Behind closed doors: video recorders in the home," in Helen Baehr and Gillian Dyer (eds) *Boxed In: Women and TV*, London: Pandora Press.

Strasser, Susan (1982) *Never Done: A History of American Housework*, New York: Pantheon.

6

I WANT THE BLACK ONE

Is there a place for Afro-American culture in commodity culture?

BEING DIFFERENT

Adults, older girls, shops, magazines, newspapers, window signs – all the world had agreed that a blue-eyed, yellow-haired, pink-skinned doll was what every girl child treasured.

(Morrison, 1970: 20)

In her powerfully compressed first novel, *The Bluest Eye*, Toni Morrison scrutinizes the influence of the white-dominated culture industry on the lives and identities of black Americans. She tells the story of three young girls: Claudia and Frieda, who are sisters, and Pecola, who comes to stay with them during a period when her own brawling parents are cast out of their store-front home. The book's setting is a working-class urban black neighborhood during the 1930s and 1940s, a time when it is already clear that American culture means white culture, and this in turn is synonymous with mass-media culture. Morrison singles out the apparently innocuous – or as Frieda and Pecola put it, "cu-ute" (Morrison, 1970: 19) – Shirley Temple, her dimpled face reproduced on cups, saucers, and baby dolls, to show how the icons of mass culture subtly and insidiously intervene in the daily lives of Afro-Americans.

Of the three girls, Claudia is the renegade. She hates Shirley Temple, and seethes with anger when she sees the blue-eyed, curly haired child actress dancing alongside the culture hero that Claudia claims for herself: Bojangles. As she sees it, "Bojangles is [her] friend, [her] uncle, [her] daddy, [and he] ought to have been soft-shoeing it and chuckling with [her]" (Morrison, 1970: 1). Claudia's intractable hostility towards Shirley Temple originates in her realization that in our society, she, like all racial "others," participates in dominant culture as a consumer, but not as a producer. In rejecting Shirley

Temple, and wanting to be the one dancing with Bojangles, Claudia refuses the two modes of accommodation that white culture holds out to black consumers. She neither accepts that white is somehow superior, thus enabling her to see Shirley Temple as a proper dancing partner for Bojangles; nor does she imagine herself miraculously translated into the body of Shirley Temple so as to vicariously live white experience as a negation of blackness. Instead, Claudia questions the basis for white cultural domination. This she does most dramatically by dismembering and tearing open the vapid blue-eyed baby dolls her parents and relatives give her for Christmas presents. Claudia's hostility is not blind, but motivated by the keen desire to get at the roots of white domination, "to see of what it was made, to discover the dearness, to find the beauty, the desirability that had escaped [her], but only [her]" (Morrison, 1970: 20).

Claudia's unmitigated rage against white culture, its dolls and movie stars, is equaled only by her realization that she could ax little white girls made of flesh and blood as readily as she rips open their plaster and sawdust replicas. The only thing that restrains Claudia from committing mayhem is her recognition that the acts of violence she imagines would be "disinterested violence" (Morrison, 1970: 22). This is an important point in Morrison's development of Claudia as the representation of a stance that Afro-Americans in general might

Photo: Karen Klugman

take against white domination. By demonstrating that violence against whites runs the risk of being "disinterested violence," Morrison suggests that white people are little more than abstractions. As the living embodiments of their culture, all white people partake of the Shirley Temple icon. To some extent, all are reified subjects, against whom it is impossible for blacks to mount passionate, self-affirming resistance or retaliation. In defining Claudia as someone who learns "how repulsive disinterested violence [is]" (Morrison, 1970: 22) Morrison affirms the fullness of her character's humanity.

Morrison's treatment of Claudia explores the radical potential inherent in the position of being "other" to dominant society. The critical nature of *The Bluest Eye* may be best appreciated when apprehended in relation to efforts by Edward Said and Franz Fanon to expose the emotionally crippling aspects of colonialism. Morrison's genius as a writer of fiction is to develop the experience of "otherness" and its denunciation in ways that were not open to either Said in *Orientalism* or Fanon in *Black Skin, White Masks*. This is because Morrison's fictional characters, while they articulate history, are not themselves bound by historical events and social structures as were Fanon's patients, whose case histories are the narrative raw material of his book. Morrison's portrayal of Pecola is the most horrifying example of the mental distortion produced by being "other" to white culture. She transforms the Fanonian model of a little black girl caught behind a white mask into a little black girl whose white mask becomes her face. Pecola's dialectical antithesis is, then, Claudia, who tears to shreds the white mask society wants her to wear.

However, Claudia's critical reversal of "otherness" is short lived. Indeed, she later learned to "worship" (Morrison, 1970: 22) Shirley Temple, knowing even as she did "that the change was adjustment without improvement" (Morrison, 1970: 22). In this, Morrison suggests that white cultural domination is far too complex to be addressed only in a retaliatory manner. A simple, straightforward response to cultural domination cannot be mounted, let alone imagined, because domination is bound up with the media, and this with commodity gratification. Claudia's desire to dance with Bojangles raises a question so crucial as to put all of American culture to the test. That is, can we conceive of mass culture as black culture? Or is mass culture by its very definition white culture with a few blacks in it? Can we even begin to imagine the media as a form capable of expressing Afro-American cultural identity?

Morrison addresses these questions by way of a parable. She tells the story of how Claudia and her sister plant a bed of marigolds and believe that the health and vigor of their seeds will ensure the health and vigor of their friend's incestuously conceived child. Morrison makes the parallel explicit: "We had dropped our seeds in our own little plot of black dirt just as Pecola's father had dropped his seeds in his own plot of black dirt" (Morrison, 1970: 9). But there were no marigolds. The seeds "shriveled and died" (Morrison, 1970: 9) as did Pecola's baby. The parable of the flower garden resonates with more meaning than the mere procreation and survival of black people. In its fullest sense, the parable asks whether we can conceive of an Afro-American cultural garden capable of bringing all its people to fruition. In the absence of a whole and sustaining Afro-American culture, Morrison shows black people making "adjustments" to mass white culture. Claudia preserves more integrity than her sister, Frieda; but both finally learn to love the white icon. Pecola magically attains the bluest eyes and with them the madness of assimilation to the white icon. Maureen, the "high-yellow dream child with long brown hair" (Morrison, 1970: 52), mimics the white icon with rich displays of fashion: "patent-leather shoes with buckles" (Morrison, 1970: 52), "colored knee socks" (Morrison, 1970: 53), and a "brown velvet coat trimmed in white rabbit fur and a matching muff" (Morrison, 1970: 53). Taken together, the four young girls represent varying degrees of distortion and denial of self produced in relation to a culture they and their parents do not make, but cannot help but consume. Can we, then, conceive of Afro-American culture capable of sustaining all four young girls, individually and collectively? And can such a culture take a mass form? To open up these questions, I want to move into the present, out of literature and into advertising, where mass-media culture has made black its "other" most frequently viewed population as compared to the less visible Asian Americans and all but invisible Hispanics.

SHOP TILL YOU DROP

I don't want to know! I just want that magical moment when I go into a store and get what I want with my credit card. I don't even want to know I'll have to pay for it.
(*Comment made by a white male student when I explained that commodity fetishism denies knowledge of the work that goes into the things we buy*)

There is a photograph by Barbara Kruger that devastatingly sums up the abstraction of self and reality in consumer society ("Untitled," 1987). The photo shows no more than a white hand whose thumb and forefinger grasp a red credit-card-like item, whose motto reads "I Shop Therefore I Am". Kruger's photograph captures the double nature of commodity fetishism as it informs both self and activity. The reduction of being to consumption coincides with the abstraction of shopping as well. This is because "using plastic" represents a deepening of the already abstract character of exchange based on money as the general equivalent.

If shopping equals mere existence, then the purchase of brand names is the individual's means of designating a specific identity. Consumer society has produced a population of corporate logo-wearers: "Esprit," "Benetton," "Calvin Klein," "Jordache," and the latest on the fashion scene, McDonald's "McKids." The stitched or printed logo is a visible detail of fashion not unlike the stickers on a banana. In the eyes of the corporate fashion industry, our function is to bring advertising into our daily lives. We may well ask whether we are any different from the old-time sandwich-board advertisers who once patrolled city streets with signs recommending "Eat at Joe's."

Until recently it was clear in the way fashion featured white models that buying a brand-name designer label meant buying a white identity. The workers who produce brand-name clothing today are predominantly Chinese, Filipino, and Mexican; or, closer to home, they are Hispanics and Asian Americans, but the corporations are as white as the interests and culture of the ruling class they maintain. The introduction of black fashion models in major fashion magazines such as *Vogue, Harper's Bazaar,* and *Glamour* may at one time have represented a potential loosening of white cultural hegemony, but this was never fully realized because high fashion circumscribes ethnic and racial identity by portraying people of color as exotic. Today, blacks appear in all forms of advertising, most often as deracinated, deculturated black integers in a white equation. This is even true in many of the advertisements one finds in such black magazines as *Ebony* and *Essence,* where the format, models, and slogans are black mirror-images of the same advertisements one sees month by month in the white magazines. For instance, in February 1988, Virginia Slims ran a magazine and billboard advertisement that featured a white model in a red and black flamenco dancing dress. Black magazines and billboards in black neighborhoods ran the same advertisement, with the same dress. The only difference was the black model inside the dress.

The question of whether or not black people can affirm identity by way of a brand name is nowhere more acutely posed than by Michael Jordan's association with "Air Nike" sports shoes. Michael Jordan *is* "Air Nike." He is not just shown wearing the shoes like some other champion might be shown eating "the breakfast of champions." Rather, his name and the brand name form a single unified logo-refrain. No other sports star, white or black, has ever attained such an intimate relationship between self and commodity. However, the personal connection between product and star does not suggest a more personalized product; rather, it speaks for the commodification of Jordan himself. Moreover, the intimate oneness between the black basketball player and the white sneaker does not represent an inroad on the white corporation, but it does ensure that thousands of black youths from 16 to 25 years of age will have a good reason for wanting hundred-dollar shoes.

A decade before Michael Jordan made black synonymous with a brand name, Toni Morrison used another of her novels to demonstrate the futility of affirming blackness with a white label. In *Song of Solomon*, Morrison depicts the anguish of Hagar, who wakes one morning to the realization that the reason for her boyfriend's lack of interest is her looks. "Look at how I look. I look awful. No wonder he didn't want me. I look terrible" (Morrison, 1977: 312). Hagar's "look" is black urban, northern, working class, with a still strong attachment to the rural south. What little connection she has to the larger white culture has been fashioned out of her mother's sweepstakes prizes and her grandmother's impulse purchases. There is nothing contrived or premeditated about Hagar and the way she spontaneously defines herself and her love for Milkman. Her boyfriend, on the other hand, is the progeny of the urban black middle class, whose forebears conquered the professions and gained access to private property. Not as fully assimilated to the brand name as Michael Jordan, Milkman, nevertheless, is a walking collection of commodities from his "cordovan leather" shoes (Morrison, 1977: 255) to his "Good cut of suit" (Morrison, 1977: 256).

In rationalizing her boyfriend's rejection of her as a fault of her "looks," Hagar assimilates race to style. She had previously been devastated by Milkman's flirtation with a woman with "penny-colored hair" and "lemon-colored skin" (Morrison, 1977: 319), and decides that in order to hold on to her boyfriend she must make herself into a less-black woman. What Hagar does not grasp is that Milkman's uncaring regard for her is an expression of his primary sexism as well as his internalized acceptance of the larger society's racist measure of blacks in terms of how closely an individual's skin and hair approximates the white model. Hagar lives her rejection as a personal affront and turns to the only means our society holds out to individuals to improve their lot and solve their problems: consumption. Hagar embodies all the pain and anxiety produced when racism and sexism permeate an intimate relationship; and she is the living articulation of consumer society's solution to racism and sexism, that is: buy a new you. Transform yourself by piling on as many brand-name styles and scents as your pocketbook will allow. The solution to a racist society is a "pretty little black skinned girl" (Morrison, 1977: 310) "who dresses herself up in the white-with-a-band-of-color skirt and matching bolero, the Maidenform brassiere, the Fruit of the Loom panties, the no-color hose, the Playtex garter belt and the Joyce con brios" (Morrison, 1977: 318); who does her face in "sunny glow" and "mango tango"; and who puts "baby clear sky light to outwit the day light on her eyelids" (Morrison, 1977: 318).

Morrison reveals her sensitive understanding of how commodity consumption mutilates black personhood when she has Hagar appear before her mother and grandmother newly decked out in the clothes and cosmetics she hauled home through a driving rainstorm: her "wet ripped hose, the soiled white dress, the sticky, lumpy face powder, the streaked rouge, and the wild wet shoals of hair" (Morrison, 1977: 318). If Hagar had indeed achieved the "look" she so desperately sought, she would only have been a black mimicry of a white cultural model. Instead, as the sodden, pitiful child who finally sees how grotesque she has made herself look, Hagar is the sublime manifestation of the contradiction between the ideology of consumer society that would have everyone believe that we all trade equally in commodities, and the reality of all marginalized people for whom translation into the dominant white model is impossible.

Morrison's condemnation of commodity consumption as a hollow solution to the problems of race, class, and gender is as final and absolute as are Hagar's subsequent delirium and death. Unable to find, let alone affirm, herself; unable to bridge the contradiction in her life by way of a shopping spree and a Cinderella transformation, Hagar falls into a fever and eventually perishes.

If consumer society were to erect a tombstone for Hagar, it would read: "Shop till you drop." This is clearly the ugliest expression ever

coined by shopping mall publicity people. Yet it is currently proclaimed with pride and glee by compulsive shoppers from coast to
coast. Emblazoned on T-shirts, bumper stickers, and flashy advertising layouts, "Shop till you drop" attests the ultimate degradation of
the consumer. How often have you heard a young woman remark,
such as the one I saw on *The Newlywed Game*, "Whenever I feel low, I
just shop till I drop!"? This is exactly what Hagar did. The difference
between Morrison's portrayal of Hagar, and the relish with which the
Newlywed contestant characterizes her shopping orgies, is Morrison's
incisive revelation of the victimization and dehumanization inherent
in mass consumption. "Shop till you drop" is a message aimed at and
accepted largely by women. (I have yet to hear a male shopper
characterize himself in such a way.) The extreme sexism of the retail
and advertising industries could not be more abusively stated.
However, the victimization, the sexism, the degradation and dehumanization all go unnoticed because the notion of consumption is
synonymous with gratification. To demonstrate the fundamental
impossibility of realizing gratification in commodity consumption, we
have only to shift the focus from consumption to production. Now I
ask you, would anyone wear a T-shirt proclaiming "Work till you
drop?" The cold fact of capitalism is that much of the workforce is
expendable. Are we to assume that a fair number of consumers are

also expendable provided they set high consumption standards on the way out?

FROM BLACK REPLICANTS TO MICHAEL JACKSON

Toni Morrison's strong condemnation of the fetishizing quality of white-dominated commodity culture is by no means unique to the tradition of black women writers. In her novel, *Meridian*, Alice Walker creates a caricature of the reification of white society that is even more grotesque than Morrison's frozen-faced white baby dolls. This is the dead white woman whose mummified body is carted about from town to town and displayed as a side-show attraction by her money-grubbing husband. In death, as was probably the case in her life, the white woman's labor power is the basis for her husband's livelihood. As a dead body, she is literally the embodiment of the congealed labor that exemplifies the commodity form. What Morrison and Walker are documenting in their portrayals of reified white characters is the consequence of the longer and deeper association with the commodity form that whites in our society have had as opposed to racial minorities. In reacting so strongly against the fetishizing power of the commodity, contemporary black women's fiction stands aghast at the level of commodity consumption that Hagar attempts in *Song of Solomon*, and suggests that total immersion in commodities is a fairly recent historical phenomenon for the broad mass of Afro-Americans. Indeed, one way to read *Song of Solomon* is as a parable of black peoples' integration with the commodity form that is depicted across the book's three female generations: from Pilate, who trades and barters for daily needs and very seldom makes a commodity purchase; to her daughter, Reba, who gets and gives a vast array of commodities that she wins rather than purchases; to Hagar, who desperately yearns for and dies because of commodities. The larger implications of Morrison's parable suggest that while the commodity form has been dominant throughout the twentieth century, daily-life economics may have been only partially commodified owing to the many social groups who, until recently, did not fully participate as consumers.

While Morrison rejects out of hand the possibility of creating a positive, affirming black cultural identity out of "sunny glow" and "mango tango," Kobena Mercer, the British film and art critic, dramatically affirms the contrary. In considering the politics of black hairstyles, Mercer defines an approach to consumer society that sees commodities giving new forms of access to black people's self-expression (Mercer, 1987). Mercer contrasts the social meanings associated with the Afro, a hairstyle popular amongst black radicals in the sixties and the general cultural movement that promoted "Black is beautiful" on into the seventies, with the conk, a hairstyle contrived during the late thirties and early forties by urban black males. Mercer sees the popular interpretation of these two hairstyles as wholly influenced by the way western culture, even since romanticism, has validated the natural as opposed to the artificial. The "Fro" was read culturally as making a strong positive statement because it was taken to represent the natural. Then, because western mythology equates the natural with the primitive – and the primitive with Africa – the "Fro" was seen as truly African, hence, the most valid form of Afro-American cultural expression. Mercer deflates all the myths by pointing out that the "Fro" was not natural but had to be specially cut and combed with a pik to produce the uniform rounded look.

Moreover, the cultural map of African hairstyles reveals a complex geography of complicated plaits and cuts that are anything but natural. Mercer's final point is that if the "Fro" was seen as natural, it was defined as such by dominant white society for whom the longer hairstyles of the late sixties meant Hippies and their version of a communal back-to-nature movement. In this way, dominant white culture assimilated the "Fro" to its meanings – including its counter-cultural meanings.

By comparision, Mercer sees the conk allowing a form of Afro-American cultural expression that was not possible with the "Fro" precisely because the conk was seen as artificial. At the time of its popularity and even on into the present, the conk has been condemned as an attempt by black men to "whiten" their appearance. Mercer gives the prevailing line of thought by citing Malcolm X on his own first conk: "on top of my head was this thick, smooth sheen of red hair – real red – as straight as any white man's . . . [the conk was] my first really big step towards self-degradation" (Mercer, 1987: 46). In contrast, Mercer's opinion of the conk is very different. As he sees it, if black men were trying to make themselves look more white and more acceptable to white ideals of style, they would not have chosen the conk. The hair was straightened by what he calls a "violent technology" and treated to produce a tight cap of glistening red to orange hair. Because of its artificiality, the conk made a radical cultural statement that cannot be inscribed in dominant racialized interpretations of culture.

> Far from an attempted simulation of whiteness I think the dye was used as a stylized means of defying the "natural" colour codes of conventionality in order to highlight artificiality and hence exaggerate a sense of difference. Like the purple and green wigs worn by black women, which Malcolm mentions in disgust, the use of red dye seems trivial: but by flouting convention with varying degrees of artifice such techniques of black stylization participated in a defiant "dandyism", fronting-out oppression by the artful manipulation of appearances.
>
> (Mercer, 1987: 47–9)

Mercer's point is finally that black culture has at its disposal and can manipulate all the signs and artifacts produced by the larger culture. The fact that these are already inscribed with meanings inherited through centuries of domination does not inhibit the production of viable culture statements, even though it influences the way such statements are read. The readings may vary depending on the historical period as well as the class, race, and gender of the reader. Mercer's own reading of the conk is facilitated by current theories in popular culture that see the commodity form as the raw material for the meanings that people produce. From this point of view, the most recognizable commodity (what is seen as wholly "artificial") is somehow freer of past associations and more capable of giving access to alternative meanings.

There is, however, an important consideration that is not addressed either by Morrison in her condemnation of commodity culture or by Mercer in his delight over the possibilities of manipulating cultural meanings. This is the way in which the dominant white culture industry produces consumable images of blacks. Considerable effort in Afro-American criticism has been devoted towards revealing racism in the images of blacks on TV and in film, but little has been written about more mundane areas such as advertising and the mass toy market. I want to suggest a hypothesis that will help us understand consumer society in a more complex way than to simply point out its racism. That is: in mass culture many of the social contradictions of capitalism appear to us as if those very contradictions had been resolved. The mass-cultural object articulates the social contradiction and its imaginary resolution in commodity form.

Witness the way in which mass culture suggests the resolution of racism.

In contrast to Morrison's Claudia, who circa 1940 was made to play with white baby dolls, black mothers in the late sixties could buy their little girls Barbie's black equivalent: Christie. Mattel marketed Christie as Barbie's friend; and in so doing, cashed in on the civil rights movement and black upward social mobility. With Christie, Mattel also set an important precedent in the toy industry for the creation of black replicants of white cultural models. The invention of Christie is not wholly unlike the inception of a black Shirley Temple doll. If the notion of a black simulacrum of Shirley Temple is difficult to imagine, this is because only recent trends in mass marketing have taught us to accept black replicants as "separate but equal" expressions of the white world. In the 1930s a black Shirley Temple would not have been possible, but if she were a 5-year-old dancing princess today, Mattel would make a doll of her in black and white and no one would consider it strange. I say this because as soon as we started to see those grotesque, sunken-chinned white "Cabbage Patch" dolls, we started to see black ones as well. Similarly, the more appealing, but curiously furry-skinned "My Child" dolls are now available in black or white and boy or girl models. Clearly, in the 1990s race and gender have become equal integers on the toy-store shelf. I know many white girls who own mass-marketed black baby dolls such as these, but I have yet to see a single little black girl with a black "Cabbage Patch" doll. What these dolls mean to little girls, both black and white, is a problem no adult should presume to understand fully, particularly as the dolls raise the questions of mothering and adoption along with race. I mention these dolls because they sum up for me the crucial question of whether it is possible to give egalitarian expression to cultural diversity in a society where the white middle class is the norm against which all else is judged. This is another way to focus the problem I raised earlier when I asked whether it is possible for Afro-American culture to find expression in a mass-cultural form.

In an essay inaugurating the new magazine *Zeta*, Bell Hooks develops the important distinction between white supremacy and older forms of racism. Hooks sees white supremacy as "the most useful term to denote exploitation of people of color in this society" (Hooks, 1988: 24) both in relation to liberal politics and liberal feminism. I would add that white supremacy is the only way to begin to understand the exploitation of black people as consumers. In contrast to racism, which bars people of color from dominant modes of production and consumption, white supremacy suggests the equalization of the races at the level of consumption. This is possible only because all the models are white. As replicants, black versions of white cultural models are of necessity secondary and devoid of cultural integrity. The black replicant ensures, rather than subverts, domination. The notion of "otherness," or unassimilable marginality, is in the replicant attenuated by its mirroring of the white model. Finally the proliferation of black replicants in toys, fashion, and advertising smothers the possibility of creating black cultural alternatives.

While the production of blacks as replicants of whites has been the dominant mass-market strategy for some twenty years, there are indications that this formula is itself in the process of being replaced by a newer mode of representation that in turn suggests a different approach to racism in society. I am referring to the look of racial homogeneity that is currently prevalent in high-fashion marketing. Such a look depicts race as no more meaningful than a blend of paint. For example, the March 1988 issue of *Elle* magazine featured a beige woman on its cover. Many more fashion magazines have since followed suit in marketing what is now called "the new ethnicity." The ethnic model who appeared on *Elle* is clearly not "a high-yellow dream child," Morrison's version of a black approximation to whiteness circa 1940. Rather, she is a woman whose features, skin tone, and hair suggest no one race, or even the fusion of social contraries. She is, instead, all races in one. A skimming perusal of *Elle*'s fashion pages reveals more beige women and a great number of white women who have been photographed in beige tones. The use of beige fashion models is the industry's metaphor for the magical erasure of race as a problem in our society. It underscores white supremacy without directly invoking the dominant race. To understand how this is achieved we have only to compare the look of racial homogeneity to the look of gender homogeneity. For some time now the fashion industry has suggested that all women, whether they are photographed in Maidenform or denim, whether they are 12 years old or 45, are equally gendered. Dominant male-defined notions about female gender, such as appear in fashion advertising, have inured many women to the possibility of gender heterogeneity. Now, the suggestion is that women with the proper "look" are equally "raced." Such a look denies the possibility of articulating cultural diversity precisely because it demonstrates that difference is only a matter of fashion. It is the new fall colors, the latest style, and the corporate logo or label, a discrete emblematic representation of the otherwise invisible white corporate godfather.

I mention *Elle*'s beige women because the fashion industry's portrayal of racial homogeneity provides an initial means of interpreting Michael Jackson, who in this context emerges as the quintessential mass-cultural commodity. Nowhere do we see so many apparent resolutions of social contradiction as we apprehend in Michael Jackson. If youth culture and expanding youth markets belie a society whose senior members are growing more numerous, more impoverished, more marginal every day, then Michael Jackson as the ageless child of 30 represents a solution to aging. If ours is a sexist society, then Michael Jackson, who expresses both femininity and masculinity but fails to generate the threat or fear generally associated with androgeny, supplies a resolution to society's sexual inequality. If ours is a racist society, then Michael Jackson, who articulates whiteness and blackness as surgical rather than cultural identities, offers an easy solution to racial conflict.

Recently I was struck when Benson, on the television show of the same name, remarked that Michael Jackson looked like Diana Ross. The show confirmed what popular opinion has been saying for some time. The comparison of Michael Jackson to Diana Ross is particularly astute when we see Jackson both as a "look" and as a music statement. Rather than defining Michael Jackson in relation to the black male music tradition, I think it makes more sense to evaluate his music with respect to black women singers – and to go much further back than Diana Ross to the great blues singers, like "Ma" Rainey, Bessie Smith, and Ethel Waters. Diana Ross and the Motown sound is in many ways the mass-cultural cancellation of the threatening remembrance of "ladies who really did sing the blues." In a path-breaking essay on the sexual politics of the blues, Hazel Carby shows how the black women blues singers attacked patriarchy by affirming women's right to mobility and sexual independence (Carby, 1986). Getting out of town and out from under a misbehaving man, refusing to be cooped up in the house, and taking the initiative in sexual relations – these are the oft-repeated themes of the black female blues tradition. By comparison, the incessant chant style developed by Diana Ross and the Supremes features refrains aimed at the containment of women's desire and the acceptance of victimization. Background percussion that delivers a chain-like sound reminiscent of slavery is an apt instrumental metaphor for lyrics such as "My world is empty without you, Babe," "I need your love, Oh, how I need your love." By physically transforming himself into a Diana Ross look-alike, Michael Jackson situates himself in the tradition of black women's blues. The thematic concerns of his music often take up the question and consequences of being sexually renegade, or "bad"; however, Jackson ultimately represents the black male reversal of all that was threatening to patriarchy in black women's blues music. Where the black women singers affirmed the right to self-determination, both economically and sexually, Jackson taunts that he is "bad" but asks for punishment. Jackson toys with the hostility associated with sexual oppression, but rather than unleashing it, he calls for the reassertion of a patriarchal form of authority.

This does not, however, exhaust the question of Michael Jackson. As the most successful Afro-American in the mass-culture industry, Jackson begs us to consider whether he represents a successful expression of Afro-American culture in mass form. To begin to answer this question we need to go back to the notion of the commodity and recognize that above all else Michael Jackson is the consummate expression of the commodity form. Fredric Jameson offers one way of understanding Michael Jackson as a commodity when he defines the contradictory function of repetition (Jameson, 1979). On the one hand, repetition evokes the endlessly reproducible and degraded commodity form itself. Jameson demonstrates how mass culture, through the production of numerous genres, forms, and styles, attempts to create the notion of newness, uniqueness, or originality. What is contradictory about repetition is that while we shun it for the haunting reminder of commodity seriality, we also seek it out. This, Jameson sees, is especially the case in popular music, where a single piece of music hardly means anything to us the first time we hear it, but comes to be associated with enjoyment and to take on personal meanings through subsequent listenings. This is because "the pop single, by means of repetition, insensibly becomes part of the existential fabric of our own lives, so that what we listen to is ourselves, our own previous auditions" (Jameson, 1979: 138).

From this point of view, we might be tempted to interpret Michael Jackson's numerous physical transformations as analogous to Ford's yearly production of its "new" models: Jackson produces a new version of himself for each concert tour or album release. The notion of a "new identity" is certainly not original to Jackson. However, the mode of his transformations and its implications define a striking difference between Michael Jackson and any previous performer's use of identity change. This is particularly true with respect to David Bowie, whose transformations from Ziggy Stardust to the Thin White Duke were enacted as artifice. Concocted out of make-up and fashion, Bowie's identities enjoyed the precarious reality of mask and costume. The insubstantial nature of Bowie's identities, coupled with their theatricality, were, then, the bases for generating disconcerting social commentary. For Jackson, on the other hand, each new identity is the result of surgical technology. Rather than a progressively developing and maturing public figure who erupts into the social fabric newly made up to make a new statement, Jackson produces each new Jackson as a simulacrum of himself, whose moment of appearance signals the immediate denial of the previous Michael Jackson. Rather than making a social statement, Jackson states himself as a commodity. As a final observation, and this is in line with Jameson's thoughts on repetition, I would say that the "original" Michael Jackson, the small boy who sang with the Jackson Five, also becomes a commodified identity with respect to the subsequent Michael Jacksons. In Jameson's words, "the first time event is by definition not a repetition of anything: it is then reconverted into repetition the second time around" (Jameson, 1979: 137). The Michael Jackson of the Jackson Five becomes "retroactively" (Jameson, 1979: 137) a simulacrum once the chain of Jackson simulacra come into being. Such a reading is a devasting cancellation of the desire for black expression in mass culture that Toni Morrison set in motion when she asked us to imagine Claudia dancing in the movies with Bojangles. This interpretation sees the commodity form as the denial of difference. All moments and modes are merely incorporated in its infinite seriality.

Commodity seriality negates the explosive potential inherent in transformation, but transformation, as it is represented culturally, need not be seen only as an expression of commodity seriality. In the black American entertainment tradition, the original metaphor for transformation, which is also a source for Michael Jackson's use of identity change, is the blackface worn by nineteenth-century minstrel performers. When, in 1829, Thomas Dartmouth Rice, a white man, blackened his face and jumped "Jim Crow" for the first time, he set in motion one of the most popular entertainment forms of the nineteenth century. By the late 1840s the Christy Minstrels had defined many of the standard routines and characters, including the cake walk and the Tambo and Bones figures that are synonymous with minstrelsy. In the 1850s and 1860s hundreds of minstrel troupes were touring the states, generally on a New York–Ohio axis. Some even journeyed to

London, where they were equally successful. By the 1880s and 1890s there were far fewer troupes, but the shows put on by the few remaining companies expanded into mammoth extravaganzas, such as those mounted by the Mastodon Minstrels.

Broadly speaking, the minstrel shows portrayed blacks as the "folk," a population wholly formed under a paternalistic southern plantation system. They were shown to be backward and downright simple-minded; they were lazy, fun-loving, and foolish; given to philandering, gambling, and dancing; they were victimized, made the brunt of slapstick humor and lewd jokes. The men were "pussy-whipped" and the woman were liars, cheats, and flirts. No wonder the minstrel shows have been so roundly condemned by Afro-American intellectuals, including Nathan Huggins, for whom the most crippling aspect of minstrelsy is the way its popularity prevented the formation of an alternative "Negro ethnic theater" (Huggins, 1971: 286). Nevertheless, a few critics have advanced the notion that minstrelsy represents a nascent form of people's culture, whose oblique – albeit distorted – reference to real plantation culture cannot be denied (Lott, 1988). It is interesting that neither position in this debate seems adequate to explain why blacks performed in minstrel shows; and why, when they did so, they too blackened their faces with burnt cork and exaggerated the shape of their lips and eyes. If the shows promoted the debasement of blacks, can black participation in them be explained by their immense popularity, or the opportunity the shows provided to blacks in entertainment, or the money a performer might make? If the shows were an early form of people's theater, was it, then, necessary for blacks in them to reiterate the racist stereotyping that blackface signified?

An initial response to these questions is provided by Burt Williams, one of the most famous black actors of this country, who joined the Ziegfield Follies against the protests of the entire white cast. Williams proved incredibly successful, earning up to $2,500 a week. Nevertheless, he chose throughout his career to perform in blackface. In their anthology of black theater, James Hatch and Ted Shine suggest that blackface was for Burt Williams "a badge of his trade, a disguise from which to work, and a positive reminder to his audience that he was a black man" (Hatch and Shine, 1974: 618). These explanations get at the motives behind Burt Williams' choice, but I suggest we consider blackface as something more than a disguise or mask, and apprehend it, instead, as a metaphor that functions in two systems of meanings. On the one hand, it is the overt embodiment of the southern racist stereotyping of blacks; but as a theatrical form, blackface is a metaphor for the commodity. It is the sign of what people paid to see. It is the image consumed and it is the site of the actor's estrangement from self into role. Blackface is a trademark and as such it can be either full or empty of meaning.

In his comprehensive study on minstrelsy, Eric Lott interprets blackface in terms of race and gender relations (Lott, 1988). He describes it as the site where all sorts of dissimulations and transformations take place that have their origin in social tensions. In blackface, white men portrayed black men. Black men portrayed white men portraying black men; and men, both black and white, became female impersonators and acted the "wench." Audiences enjoyed flirting with the notion of actually seeing a black man perform on stage, when such was generally not allowed. And they enjoyed the implications of seeing men put themselves in the bodies of women so as to enact sexual affairs with other men. Blackface allowed the transgression of sexual roles and gender definition even while it disavowed its occurrence. As Eric Lott points out, minstrelsy was highly inflected with the desire to assume the power of the "other," even while such power was being denigrated and denied. As he puts it, minstrelsy was "a derisive celebration of the power of blacks" (and, I would add, women too) which is contained within the authority of the white male performer. So, on the one hand, blackface is heavily laden with overt racist and sexist messages; but, on the other, it is hollowed of social meanings and restraints. This makes blackface a site where the fear of miscegenation can be both expressed and managed, where misogyny can be affirmed and denied, and where race and gender can be stereotyped and transgressed.

The contradictory meanings of mistrelsy offer another way of looking at Michael Jackson, who from this perspective emerges as the embodiment of blackface. His physical transformations are his trademark – a means of bringing all the sexual tensions and social contradictions present in blackface into a contemporary form. From this perspective, Jackson's artistic antecedent is not Diana Ross, or even Burt Williams, but the great black dancer Juba, who electrified white audiences with his kinetic skill which had people seeing his body turned back to front, his legs turned left to right. While Juba performed in blackface, his body was for him yet a more personal means for generating parody and ironic self-dissimulation. Juba's "Imitation Dance" offered his highly perfected rendition of each of the blackfaced white actors who had defined a particular breakdown dance, as well as an imitation of himself dancing his own consummate version of breakdown. This is the tradition that best defines Michael Jackson's 1989 feature-length video, *Moonwalker*. Here, Jackson includes video versions of himself as a child singing and dancing the Motown equivalent of breakdown; he then ricochets this "real" image of himself off the image of a contemporary child impersonator who imitates Jackson in dress, face, song, and dance; and, finally, bounces these versions off a dozen or so other memorable Jackson images – his teen years, Captain EO – who are preserved on video and appear like so many Jackson personae or masks. In fading from one version of Jackson to the next, or splicing one Jackson against another, *Moonwalker* represents transformation as formalized content. Not surprisingly, most of the stories on the video are about transformation – a theme stunningly aided by the magic of every cinematic special effect currently available.

In opening her analysis of the sambo and minstrel figures, Sylvia Wynter states that the "imperative task" of black culture is "transformation" (Wynter, 1979: 149). Wynter's optimistic account of the power of stigmatized black and popular culture to create a system of subversive counter-meanings leads her to see minstrelsy as the place where black culture "began the cultural subversion of the normative bourgeois American reality" (Wynter, 1979: 155). Michael Jackson's *Moonwalker* opens with the desire for equally sweeping social change. The initial piece, "Man in the Mirror," surveys the faces of the world's disinherited, vanquished, and famished people, along with their often martyred benefactors: Gandhi, Mother Teresa, the Kennedy brothers, Martin Luther King, Jr; against those are counterposed the images of fascist oppressors from Hitler to the Klan. The message of the song, hammered home to the beat of the refrain, is that if you want to change the world, begin with the "Man in the Mirror". That the desire for social change is deflected into multitudinous self-transformations is to varying degrees the substance of all the video narratives assembled in *Moonwalker*. Two of these specifically demonstrate how blackface is redefined in the rubric of contemporary commodity culture.

In "Smooth Criminal," the grease and burnt cork that turned the minstrel artist into "Jim Crow" or "Zip Coon" are replaced by the metallic shell and electronic circuitry that turn Michael Jackson into a larger than life transformer robot. The story has Michael Jackson pitted against a depraved white drug lord bent on taking over the world by turning all young children (white and black; boys and girls) into addicts. The drug lord is aided by an army of Gestapo-like troops, reminiscent of the stormtroopers from *Star Wars*. At the story's climactic moment, the army encircles Jackson, trapping him in the depths of their drug factory hideaway. Writhing on the floor under a relentless spotlight, completely surrounded by the faceless army, Michael Jackson is caught in a setting that dramatically summons up a parallel image: the rock star, alone on the stage in an immense stadium where he is beseiged by a wall of faceless fans. The emblematic similarity between the story of persecution and subjugation and the experience of rock stardom establishes a connection to the minstrel tradition, where the theater was the site for enacting the forms of domination and their potential transformation.

Jackson's submission to the forces of domination is broken when the drug lord begins to beat a little girl whom he has kidnapped and whose cries push Jackson to the brink of superhuman action. Suddenly, Jackson's face, already tightly stretched over surgically sculpted bones becomes even more taut; indeed, metallic. His eyes lose their pupils, glow, and become lasers. Jackson rises and a control box pops out of his stomach. His feet and arms sprout weapons. Michael Jackson is a robot. The transformation makes a stunning commentary on all Jackson's real-life physical transformations that *Moonwalker* cites, and suggests that robotics is the logical next step in medical technology's reshaping of the human body.

However, the most powerful implication of Jackson's transformation – one that every child will grasp – is that Michael Jackson has made himself into a commodity. He is not a generic robot, but specifically a transformer. This Jackson demonstrates when he subsequently transforms himself from robot warrior into an armed space vehicle. In this shape, he ultimately vanquishes the drug lord. In a previous chapter I developed the significance of transformers as metaphors of gendering under capitalism. Jackson's assimilation to transformer includes the erasure of gender traits simultaneous with the assumption of absolute male sexual potency. The transformer represents industrial technology in commodity form. If in the United States industry and the market are controlled by a largely white male hierarchy, then Jackson's transformation figurally raises the question of social power relationships. The question is whether Jackson, in becoming a transformer, appropriates an image associated with white male economic and sexual domination or whether he has been assimilated to the image. Is this a case of usurping power, or has Jackson, as "other," merely been absorbed? Another way to look at this question is to ask whether the appropriation of the commodity form is in any way analogous to previous instances where blacks have appropriated white cultural forms. We might substitute religion for the commodity and ask some of the same questions. Has religion, commencing with colonization and the slave trade, functioned as an ideological arm of white domination; or does the appropriation of religion by the black church represent the reverse of colonization, where blacks denied salvation claimed God for their own? We are back to the dilemma that I initially posed with reference to Toni Morrison, who might well argue that the transformer represents a form of colonization even more dehumanizing than that embodied by the blue-eyed Pecola because in it race and gender are wholly erased. In contrast, Kobena Mercer might be tempted to see the transformer as today's equivalent of the conk.

As if in response, and to consider the commodity from yet another angle, Michael Jackson enacts another parable of transformation. In "Speed Demon," the video wizards employ the magic of "clay-mation" to turn Michael Jackson into a Brer Rabbit figure, whose invisible popular culture referent is, of course, Gumby. "He was one a little green blob of clay, but you should see what Gumby can do today." This is a refrain familiar to childhood TV audiences of the early seventies in the United States. The song is about transformation from blob of clay to boy, making Gumby a proto-transformer. Indeed, Gumby's boyish degendering corresponds with the erasure of gender traits that we see in the transformers. His body absolutely smooth and malleable, Gumby's only noticeable features are his big eyes and rubbery mouth. If gender is deemphasized, Gumby's green hue suggests possible racial otherness. Bear in mind that Gumby coincides with the advent of *Sesame Street*, where multiracial and multicultural neighborhoods are depicted by collections of multicolored humans, monsters, and animals. Purple, yellow, green, and blue are the colors of *Sesame Street*'s Rainbow Coalition.

"Speed Demon" reworks the themes of pursuit and entrapment in a theatrical setting that parallels, although in a more light-hearted way, the portrayal of these themes in the transformer script. In this case Michael Jackson is pursued by overly zealous fans, who, during the course of a movie studio tour, recognize him and chase him through various lots and sound stages. The fans are grotesquely depicted as clay animations with horribly gesticulating faces and lumpy bodies. At one point Jackson appears to be cornered by a host of frenzied fans, but manages to slip into a vast wardrobe building where he discovers a full head mask of a rather goofy, but sly-looking rabbit. At this point, Jackson undergoes "claymation" transformation. This completely redefines the terms of his relationship to his pursuers. "Claymation" turns Michael Jackson into a motorcycle-riding Brer Rabbit, the trickster of the Afro-American folk tradition who toys with the oppressors, outsmarts them, outmaneuvers them – and with glee! The Speed Demon is Gumby, he is Brer Rabbit, and he is also most definitely Michael Jackson, whose "wet curl" look caps the clay head of the rabbit, and whose trademark dance, the "moonwalk," is the rabbit's particular forte.

At the tale's conclusion, Michael, having eluded his pursuers, greets the sunrise in the California desert. Here he removes the rabbit disguise, which at this point is not the "claymation" body double but a simple mask and costume that Jackson unzips and steps out of. But lo and behold, the discarded costume takes on a life of its own and becomes a man-sized, moonwalking rabbit who challenges Jackson to a dancing duel. In a video rife with transformations and doublings, this is the defining instance. In dance, the vernacular of black cultural expression, the conflict between the artist and his exaggerated, folksy, blackface alter ego is enacted (Hebdige, 1987). Like Juba dancing an imitation of himself, Michael Jackson separates himself from his blackface and out-moonwalks the commodity form of himself.

In posing transformation as the site at which the desire for black cultural autonomy coincides with the fetishization of commodity capitalism, *Moonwalker* denies commodity seriality. Instead, it defines the commodity form in the tradition of blackface as the nexus of struggle. The cultural commodity is not neutral, but instead defines a zone of contention where the terms of cultural definition have been largely determined by the white male-dominated system of capitalist production, and reified by the fetishizing nature of the commodity itself.

In my accounts of "Smooth Criminal" and "Speed Demon," I suggest that some commodity manifestations provide more room for counter-statements than others. The transformers are so closely associated with high-tech capitalism that they offer little opening other than the ambiguity over appropriation versus assimilation. By comparison, the complex relationship between Gumby, Brer Rabbit, and Michael Jackson creates a space where the collision between black vernacular and mass-media forms suggests the subversion of domination. "Speed Demon" deconstructs the commodity form, and with it, Michael Jackson as well, who by the end of the video emerges as a multiple subject reflected back from a dozen commodified mirror-images. *Moonwalker* engages with commodity fetishism and opens up the commodity form, but does it provide a platform for the emergence of what Stuart Hall calls the "concrete historical subject" (Hall, 1986)? Is there a Meridian in this text, capable of discovering a self out of the social fragments and conflicts? Can anything approaching the autonomous subject be discerned in this text? *Moonwalker* suggests a split between contemporary black women's fiction, which strives to create images of social wholeness based on the rejection of commodity capitalism, and what seems to be a black male position which sees the commodity as something that can be played with and enjoyed or subverted. Where Michael Jackson tricks the commodity form, and is able to do so precisely because its meanings are fetishized and therefore not culturally specific, Alice Walker refuses commodity fetishism and, in *The Color Purple*, imagines a form of cottage industry that has Celie organizing the collective production of customized pants for her extended community of family and friends. Jackson reaches back into the culture industry to minstrelsy and seizes blackface, updates it in contemporary forms, and unites himself with the history of black male actors who were made and unmade by their relationship to the commodity. Contrarywise, Alice Walker looks back upon commodity production, sees its earliest manifestation in the "slops" produced for slaves (Ewen and Ewen, 1982: 167), its continuation in the fashion industry that destroyed Morrison's Hagar, and summarily denies the possibility of the mass-produced commodity as having anything to offer Afro-Americans.

MINSTRELSY: THE DISNEY VERSION

If, as a cultural commodity, Michael Jackson occasionally opens the commodity form to reveal its contradictory subtexts, this is not necessarily the case in the culture industry as a whole. Indeed, it is a rarity. Most often, the commodity effaces contradiction by compressing its varied and potentially contradictory subtexts into a single homogenized and ahistorical form. To demonstrate what I mean, and to underscore the potentially radical discontinuities that Michael Jackson articulates in *Moonwalker*, I want to cite another figure from mass culture who is even more popular than Michael Jackson and who embodies the compression of contradiction in commodity form. I am referring to Mickey Mouse. The scandalous point I want to make is that Mickey Mouse is black; indeed, a minstrel performer. Of course, at the same time, he is quite simply Mickey Mouse, the most famous mass-cultural icon, born of Walt Disney's entrepreneurial genius and, as a commodity, laundered of all possible social and historical associations. Nevertheless, the original Mickey Mouse was often portrayed dancing an erratic jig: animation's version of what it must have been like to jump "Jim Crow." Then too, the escapades and narrow escapes that typify Mickey's early cartoons closely resemble those found in the "pickaninny" cartoons from the same and a somewhat later period. In fact, Mickey's physical features: scrawny black body, big head, big mouth, differ from those of the pickaninny only in the substitution of big ears for kinky hair. The pickaninny cartoons invariably showed a black baby being chased and swallowed by alligators, hippos, lions, and other beasts with cavernous mouths. These are the sight gags that Mickey Mouse reverses in his debut film, *Steamboat Willie*. Instead of being swallowed, Mickey beats a tune out of a cow's teeth and twangs a goat's tongue. Significantly, the tune is "Turkey in the Straw," a melody originally sung by George Washington Dixon, an early blackface performer.

The fact that I can tease out references to minstrelsy in "Steamboat Willie" and establish comparisons between Mickey, whose black body is not stated as race, and the pickaninnies, whose black bodies signified race, testifies to the partial iconographic commodification of the 1929 version of Mickey Mouse. I doubt whether any of these buried referents can be brought out of the bland, big-cheeked Mickey of the sixties, whose morphological development from rat to baby-faced mouse is the subject of an interesting essay by the popular science writer Stephen J. Gould (1982). Nevertheless, submerged references to minstrelsy were evoked as late as the 1950s by two other cartoon figures: Heckle and Jeckle, a pair of magpies whose plumes are the naturalized equivalent of the black tail-feathers that Burt Williams wore to emphasize racist stereotyping. There is yet another buried minstrel subtext in the depiction of Heckle and Jeckle. In their particular magpie loquaciousness, the way the birds practiced verbal one-upmanship, Heckle and Jeckle recreate two stock minstrel figures: Mr Tambo and Mr Bones. Where Heckle and Jeckle are invariably shown perched on a branch and "signifying" at each other, Tambo and Bones stood at opposite ends of the minstrel line of players. From these positions, they bantered back and forth through the straw-dog mediator: the "interlocutor." By its very nature, the commodity form – and particularly the mass media commodity as compared with earlier forms of commodified entertainment – reduces the historical specificity of its referential material and combines a tremendous array of cultural sources. Besides being minstrel players, Heckle and Jeckle are also Jekyll and Hyde. And finally, they are simply Heckle and Jeckle, two magpies invented by Terry Toons. The advent of cultural icons such as Mickey Mouse and Heckle and Jeckle signals the moment at which it is no longer possible to distinguish the historical subtexts at the point of consumption. Mickey Mouse came to the screen some twenty to thirty years after the height of the minstrel tradition. Indeed, as a cultural commodity, Mickey Mouse is finally not black. He is precisely the cancellation of the black cultural subtext, and quite possibly the "retroactive" eradication of the original minstrel performer who jumped "Jim Crow" to the tune of "Turkey in the Straw." This first-time event, now apprehended from the cultural moment defined by Mickey Mouse, is, then, redefined as a simulacrum of the Disney tradition.

We might unwrap and unpack all our homogenized commodity icons as I have done with Mickey Mouse in order to reveal how each and every one compresses and negates social contradictions. However, the deconstruction of commodities is not a transformation of the social and economic inequalities inherent in commodity capitalism. Or, like Toni Morrison and Alice Walker, we might reject the commodity for its reification of human qualities and cancellation of cultural difference, and attempt, as they do in their novels, to imagine utopian social relationships. Such a strategy has the potential to estrange the racism and sexism that are internalized in relationships, so that these can be apprehended critically. However, this approach risks essentializing, if not blackness, then a rural over an urban experience or a previous historical period, such as the thirties or forties, over the present. Or, like Michael Jackson, we might fully assume the commodity, and with every act or cultural statement stake the risk of absolute reification against the possibility of generating transcendent cultural images. This approach fully relinquishes a connection to the social for the sake of developing control over the image as a commodity. All these strategies are partialities, and can only be so, in a system where the totalizing factor is the commodity form.

7

SWEET DREAMS
Profits and payoffs in commodity capitalism

Could commodities themselves speak, they would say: In the eyes of each other we are nothing but exchange values.

(Marx, *Capital*, vol. I)

SUGAR: PURE POISON

During the seventies, as a watershed of the ecology movement, when health food all but merged with mainstream eating habits, a number of anti-sugar books hit the health-food circuit, then came to the attention of the wider public. One of these is William Dufty's *Sugar Blues*, a century-by-century exposé that attributes all the world's health problems to poisonous refined sugar. These include beriberi, scurvy, schizophrenia, pellagra, lung cancer, and of course diabetes. According to Dufty, the introduction of sugar into people's diets has always coincided with the impoverishment of traditionally wholesome food regimes. Sugar is the alimentary chemistry of colonialism. For instance, the British brought beriberi to Java when their polished white rice and sugar supplanted the nutrient-rich native brown rice, just as the Americans destroyed their allies, the South Vietnamese, with instant Minute Rice and Coca Cola while the Viet Cong prevailed on unrefined rice and a bit of salt.

The common line in Dufty's book, as in all the anti-sugar writing of the period, is heavily moralizing. Not only is sugar shown to be a means of colonial domination, it is also the repository of western guilt: guilt over slavery, guilt over indulgent childrearing practices; guilt over commodity glut and consumption in general. Having a sweet tooth is the sin of the west, while obesity is the bodily condemnation of those who have sinned. One very interesting study of the anti-sugar writing sees it as a backlash against the counter-cultural promiscuity of the sixties (Mechling and Mechling, 1983). In this case, sugar is the metaphoric replacement for the unnamed modes of disorderly conduct more generally associated with the sixties: drugs and sex. The stand against sugar is, thus, a call for a moral return to social order.

The moral dimension of Dufty's criticism makes his book broadly appealing. It rouses the reader's passion in a way similar to soap opera and romance. Moralizing is the basis of the book's strength, but it can also reveal the shortcomings of Dufty's approach as a method for cultural criticism in general. To show what I mean, I will focus on one of the book's anecdotes. Dufty tells the story of a young man, who, upon graduation from high school, is diagnosed as diabetic. His family had a history of diabetes and hypoglycemia. As a child, he had watched his grandmother giving herself insulin injections. But sugar, as a convenient and gratifying component of the family's daily diet, was something neither he nor his mother ever questioned. Indeed, this young man grew up during the era when children were taught to do their duty to the meat and potatoes on their plates so as to get to the Jello, the pudding, or the Betty Crocker cake. Today, sugar is not confined to dessert, but is available for consumption at all hours: the coffee-break donut, the schoolyard granola bar snack, the McDonald's lunch, the 4:00 p.m. Snickers bar, and late-night TV-viewing munchies.

Dufty's account of the 18-year-old diabetic summons up an image of the nuclear family, a mother who did not work outside the home, and family members who sat down to meals together. The story is poignant for those who feel nostalgia for the nuclear family and guilt over its demise. The story is about a young man, but it is aimed at the mothers of this world. The young man emerges as the embodiment of the larger culture of compulsive consumption and the mother's ignorant dotage. Out of love, the mother and grandmother have fed the young man sweets. They are the perpetrators of his victimization.

Dufty's account of the young man reaches its climax on the evening following his diagnosis. This is the night before he will begin the life-long daily process of injecting insulin. He is about to turn himself into a chemical monitoring system, whose highs and lows have the potential to kill him. On this night his mother visits him in his room and in the context of sorrow, guilt, and Oedipal tensions she gives him a Hershey bar: his last. This is how Dufty hammers home his point about the feminine weakness of people who overindulge in sugar. The moralizing approach to consumption sees the individual as victim, someone out of control and unquestioning. To be a sugar addict is to be a woman or a child, a guileless dupe, easily led, and predisposed to indulgence. A few tough-minded individuals have the strength to go "cold turkey," kick sugar addiction, and then rebuke the rest of us for our laxity. This, of course, means Dufty himself, who represents the masculine stance toward weakness and overindulgence. His mission is salvation through pedagogy. He will teach us how we too can take control over our lives and become sugar-free.

The moralizing approach reduces everything to the individual. This makes it inadequate as a basis for cultural criticism. Very little attention is given to the social and economic forces that determine what gets produced and sold, how new commodity markets are formed, how these are influenced by the ideology of progress, and the sort of struggles that have erupted over consumption. Instead, consumption is portrayed as a matter of good or bad choices made by weak or strong individuals. Dufty does mention protracted opposition in Britain to the use of sugar in brewing beer, and he describes early legal action taken against the sale of Coca Cola over state lines. But for the most part the consumer is portrayed as a pawn to the sugar industry and the conspiratorial "diseasestablishment" ("That part of the establishment – once minor, now major – which profits directly and indirectly, legally and illegally, from human misery and malaise": Dufty, 1976: 44). This brings us to another aspect of the moralizing approach to cultural criticism: the tendency to cast the forces of capitalism as conspiratorial. This is symptomatic of the individual's initial realization that capitalism puts profits before people. Such an interpretation may serve as impetus to class consciousness as it replaces the individual's sense of particularity and dramatically redefines history as "them versus us." But conspiracy does not provide a means of understanding the complex struggles and social relationships within capitalism that, even though they have promoted profit-making at the expense of the working class, cannot be conceived in a singularly polarized way.

Wholly left out of the moralizing/conspiratorial approach to culture are the social meanings of commodities and the choices we make as consumers. As Dufty sees us, we are all weak but, nevertheless, free to learn how to make proper choices. These require shopping at only the purest health-food establishments (many not so pure ones push heavily brown-sugared baked goods) and generally switching to traditional Japanese cuisine. Dufty does not question the cultural meanings embedded in such practices. In our society shopping in health-food stores and adopting foreign cuisines are activities that are highly defined by class and that have strong student and professional white middle-class associations. The other area of meaning that Dufty does not confront, although it is implied in his anecdotes, is the powerful cultural connection between sugar and sex; or, in a modified version, between sugar and love, sentiment, nurture, and care. Dufty condemns the Fannie Farmer Cookbook because it taught young American girls that the way to win and keep a man was to bake him delicious pies and cakes. But the moralizing approach can go no further. It dispenses with the complexity of meanings associated with commodities and the way in which commodities enter into human discourse. The mother of the 18-year-old diabetic who gives her child his last Hershey bar is complicitous with the "diseasestablishment." But she is also expressing her love in the standard code of commodity meanings. She might have chosen to give her child a more elite brand of chocolate – say, Godiva – for his last sweet indulgence, but this would have altered their moment of being together. The family has traded and based their communication on standard brand names. The Godiva chocolate would have ruptured that communication by making obvious reference to a social class to which mother and son do not belong. In giving her child a Hershey bar, the mother has chosen the top of the standard line – not the cut-rate bargain variety, or the homemade version (both would have had other social meanings). Her choice is in keeping with her son's past relationship to the food industry and his future relationship to the drug industry (insulin, like chocolate, is marketed as a standard brand).

We all make meanings with the commodities we use and bestow. But the meaning possibilities are already inscribed in the history of commodity production and exchange. The school of popular culture criticism that promotes meaning-making as the redemptive aspect of our relationship to a commodified culture sometimes goes so far as to imply that we can make wholly new meanings. It is as if the mother might lift the Hershey bar out of history so that its only meanings were those that she and son chose to give it. Of course, she might have chosen not to give her son a Hershey bar – not to give him anything at all. Such a choice might suggest abdication to the new commodity – the insulin that they are going to buy in the morning; or it might represent the possibility of an alternative relationship, one where commodities do not bear the burden of unspoken words and feelings. In this case, the mother would have had to go to her son's room empty-handed and ready to talk. For a family whose communication has been mediated by the commodity form, the possibility of an unmediated social relationship might be terrifying. The allegory of the Hershey bar begs scrutiny of how commodities enter into our most caring relationships and how they condition the meanings we make. The moralizing approach that defines sugar as poison and the "diseasestablishment" as conspiracy recognizes meaning only at the level of choice: brown rice versus sugar; strength versus weakness. It presumes that more complex relationships to the commodity do not exist.

SUGAR: PURE PROFITS

In contrast to the health-foodist critique of sugar, there is another, wholly different, body of research aimed at establishing the relationship between sugar and the political economy of capitalism. This approach uncovers other forms of moralizing and includes its own tendency toward evoking conspiracy. The most comprehensive study along these lines is Sidney Mintz's *Sweetness and Power*. Drawing on the work of eminent economic historians, Mintz demonstrates that sugar was crucial to capital accumulation and to the formation of new social classes. The most provocative aspect of Mintz's study is the implication that the erosion of the health of the working class, brought about by the widespread consumption of sugar, was in the interests of capitalism.

At one point, Mintz cites the Atlantic trade historian R. J. Davis, who observed: "By 1750 the poorest English farm labourer's wife took sugar in her tea" (Mintz, 1985: 45). I want to look at Davis' words from a number of angles because a lot is said in this otherwise simple and direct statement. First of all, like everything that pertains to the history of commodities, the rate of sugar consumption in 1750 is not culturally marked. We do not commemorate what may well be the advent of the mass-commodity market. This is not one of those dates we all learned in school, like 1492. Nevertheless, it is as significant in the formation of global capitalism as was Columbus' voyage to the Americas. In claiming, colonizing, and turning the Caribbean basin into what amounted to a factory for the production of tropical commodities, Europe created the wellspring of economic accumulation that was essential to the subsequent development of industry and wage labor in the core states. Sugar consumption defined for the first time on a broad scale a mass market of commodity consumers who were themselves entering the ranks of wage labor, and whose lives and potential to produce were inextricably linked to the distant, and to them invisible, mass of slave laborers. The lives of the latter were all but forfeit even while their potential to produce was dependent on commodities made by European workers and shipped to the plantations; and while their continued bondage (whether slavery or indentured labor) was ensured by the level of sugar consumption of those same European workers. This is the circuit of global capitalism, where the lives and livelihoods of the least advantaged producer/consumers are interdependent, but not understood by them to be so; and where the relationship between these most disadvantaged sectors enables almost infinite profit-making by a diverse capitalist class, in this case composed of investors, speculators, shippers, processors, wholesalers, government officials, retailers, and plantation owners.

I think it is safe to say that no other single source has generated profits equal to that of the sugar economy, although it may today be rivaled by the drug trade. Even the wealth of Aztec and Inca gold was of less significance to the overall economic transformation of Europe than was sugar and its companion commodities: tea and coffee. There is some dispute between economic historians as to whether or not capitalism existed at the inception of the sugar trade. Some would argue that the capital accumulation produced in the colonies made possible the later advent of capitalism as an industrial mode in Europe. The controversy focuses on the economic status of slave labor. Dependency economic theorists, such as Immanuel Wallerstein, maintain that slavery is indeed compatible with capitalism as the mode of labor control developed in the periphery. Wallerstein emphasizes a necessary link between the highly exploited labor in the periphery and the inception of wage labor in the core, a link that Marx corroborates: "The veiled slavery of wage workers of Europe needed for its pedestal, slavery pure and simple in the New World."

On a somewhat different line of reasoning, C. L. R. James has pointed to the high degree of organization that typified Caribbean slavery and the exacting temporal demands required in sugar production as initial manifestations of a capitalist mode of production (James, 1963: 392). Both James and Wallerstein agree that large-scale, single-crop production for a global market is a feature that commonly difines the Third World in global capitalism. Contrary-wise, the Trinidadian historian Eric Williams takes the more traditional position that capitalism comes into being only with wage labor and the particular way in which "free" labor allows for the creation of surplus value. For Williams, slavery and colonialism generated the wealth that made it possible for capitalism to develop in Europe (William, 1964).

What I find interesting in the debate over whether or not slavery is a capitalist mode of labor is the emphasis that economic historians place on production and the relative lack of attention they pay to consumption. For in the way that sugar articulates an economic relationship between coerced and "free" laborers, and defines both as consumers of commodities, sugar exemplifies commodity capitalism. That the Aztec gold was of a lesser economic significance to European capitalism has largely to do with the fact that it was a luxury item. It could be hoarded in the hands of the few. It never entered or created a mass-commodity market. In contrast, sugar was immensely profitable and it had a tremendous effect on the structure of European economics precisely because it left the hands of the few and became a commodity for the mass market. A high price paid by the wealthy few does not provide the overall capital gain that a lower price paid by the masses does. Moreover, the wider the distribution of a commodity, the more sites it creates for profit-making. These are the lessons that sugar offered the incipient capitalist classes of Europe. They are borne out in the history of its consumption. Demand for sugar doubled, then quadrupled during the eighteenth century (Deerr, 1950: 532). By the nineteenth century, as Sidney Mintz puts it, sugar had become "the first mass produced exotic necessity of a proletarian working class" (Mintz, 1985: 46).

The notion of an "exotic necessity" may initially seem odd. We might be tempted to think of all the now exotic commodities, such as kiwi fruit, on their way to becoming staples in the mass diet. As I pointed out in chapter 3, this is indeed the case. While all Third World commodities have the potential to become standard fare, sugar went one step further to become a necessity. What seems to be an oxymoron in Mintz's statement is instead an interesting device to focus attention on the historical transformation of sugar from an "exotic" or luxury item available only to the privileged classes to a daily "necessity" of the working class as their main source of calories. We might say that the need for a quantum leap in capital accumulation was met by sugar production, while the greatly increased energy needs of the European workforce were met by the introduction and increasing use of sugar in working-class diets. In detailing the expansion of sugar consumption in Britain, Mintz demonstrates that the general diet of most people was at the same time declining in nutritional value. Throughout the eighteenth century, sugar and a few other new, but non-nutritional substances (tobacco, coffee, tea) were the only major additions to the English diet (Mintz, 1985: 149). One example of capitalism's exploitation of the wage labor workforce was the failure to expand the production of grains and other food-stuffs, coupled with the use of sugar as a substitute for nutrition and a ready source of short-term energy. White bread and jam, tea and sugar: this was the subsistence diet of many women and children in the mid-nineteenth century. Without the "exotic necessities," their diet would have amounted to bread and water.

Social commentators, many of them clerics, in the late eighteenth and early nineteenth centuries generally deplored the eating habits of the poor and working class. Their condemnations are little different from those hurled by William Dufty against contemporary sugar addicts. The eighteenth-century poor were seen as indolent and slothful, too lazy to prepare more substantial food, and too easily led by a passion for sweets. The writing is full of moralizing epithets. Sugar and tea were labeled as "drugs" overindulged upon by the "meanest" laborers and the "lowest of the people" (Mintz, 1985: 114). Mintz cites only one authoritative voice from the end of the late eighteenth century, a cleric, David Davies, who grasped the economic reality that gave the lie to his colleagues' reproachful moralizing:

> You exclaim tea is a luxury. If you mean fine hyson tea, sweetened with refined sugar, and softened with cream, I readily admit it to be so. But this is not the tea of the poor. Spring-water, just coloured with a few leaves of the lowest-priced tea, and sweetened with the brownest sugar, is the luxury for which you reproach them. To this they have recourse of necessity, . . . tea-drinking is not the cause, but the consequence of the distress of the poor.
>
> (Mintz, 1985: 115)

The cleric is indeed astute, for he goes on to reveal one of the central contradictions of colonial economics, when he remarks that the common folk of Europe could not afford to buy the foods produced on their own soil, but could sustain themselves on the non-foods (tea and sugar) "imported from opposite sides of the earth" (Mintz, 1985: 116). The same holds true today as research indicates that the working class and poor consume more sugar than the middle classes.

In the same way that eighteenth-century theologians rebuked the poor for their dietary habits, many commentators today deplore the cultural choices made by teenagers, women, children, or the mass audience in general. (You will note that men are seldom isolated as a group and reproached in the same way, except by some brands of feminist criticism.) Such groups are credited with having no taste, being easily led, or bought off for the price of a cheap fix. Moralizing finds its way into criticism because culture in capitalist society is lived personally. In chapter 1 I mentioned that it is very difficult to conjure up images of the past without summoning up the bugaboo of nostalgia. Likewise, it is difficult to make observations concerning habits of consumption without triggering a moral response. I admit to stomach-churning revulsion when I walk into a 9:00 a.m. class and find half the students initiating their daily caloric intake with a can of Classic Coke: their only breakfast. I might, like the eighteenth-century clerics who condemned the poor for their dependence on sugar, rebuke the students as junk-food junkies. Such moralizing superiority merely betrays my generation's habits, which were formed by a less developed commodity market than exists today. The point that needs to be made is that there is no appreciable difference between their Coke and my coffee, either in terms of the economics of commodity consumption or the history of addictive commodity stimulants. The original bitter–sweet combination of tropical ingredients in Coke: cola nut, a stimulant; cocaine, an addictive agent; and sugar, habituating, appeasing, and stimulating, simply recreate the well-proven formula for mass market and profits that sugared tea and coffee defined in the eighteenth century. Coke is more modern than its predecessors: a fully processed and packaged commodity whose ingredients, derived from widely separate regions of the formerly colonized world, are mixed by the corporation to standardized specification. Some may interpret Coke's abandonment of cocaine as a choice made in the consumer's interest: but it probably has more to do with the economics of an already established mass-commodity market where there is little need for a more powerful addictive hook than the habit-forming combination of caffeine and sugar. Similarly, Coke's current use of corn syrup as a sweetener rather than sucrose (refined sugar) hardly represents an upgrading of nutritional standards. As Coke sheds its basic ingredients, it becomes a postmodern simulacrum of itself. Decaffeinated and sweetened with Nutra-Sweet, it suits the negligible energy and stimulation needs of a workforce that spends eight hours a day feeding information into a machine. If capitalism was once able to sustain a workforce on a poor diet, rich only in calories, it now does so on a diet diminished in calories.

Without going so far as to call the forces of capitalism a "diseas-establishment," Mintz nevertheless describes the deleterious effect of sugar on the health of the working class in such a way that the implication of conspiracy lurks between the lines of his analysis. This he directly disclaims by saying: "There was no conspiracy at work to wreck the nutrition of the British working class, to turn them into addicts, or ruin their teeth" (Mintz, 1985: 186). Indeed, one need not prove conspiracy on the part of sugar brokers, government officials, and plantation owners in order to recognize the profits and payoffs that sugar garnered to capitalism. Understanding the history of sugar production and its role in the formation of a mass market is itself an indictment of commodity capitalism. Conspiracy just is not the right word. Capitalists as individuals did not plot directly – or even covertly – to achieve the well-defined goals that Mintz enumerates. Neverthe-less, the forces of capitalism brought about the dependency of the working class on cheap stimulants, the maintenance of working-class energy balanced against the erosion of general health and longevity, and an immensely profitable system of production and consumption. Rather than conspiracy, a better way to conceptualize what sugar has meant to capitalism is to see it in terms of its payoffs. The formation of a mass-commodity market for the satisfaction of daily needs in such a way as to establish the control of the working class is the least recognized and most consequential payoff of the sugar economy.

Sometimes literature can give better insight into the complexities of commodity capitalism than can economic or theoretical analysis. This may be because we as readers are more able to accept and detect multivalent relationships and motives in literary characters than we believe possible in individuals constituted as representatives of particular classes. No one more poignantly portrays the connection between sugar and capitalism and its implications for black Americans than does Toni Morrison.

In *Song of Solomon*, Morrison uses sugar to show how the commodity as payoff puts those who are most exploited in a position of being complicitous with their exploitation. In the novel, Guitar remembers his father's gruesome death: sawn in half lengthwise at the sawmill where he worked. What makes the death traumatic for Guitar is, in part, the manner of his father's death, which is Morrison's way of summing up all the violence done to blacks as laborers, and in part, the manner of his burial, "boxed backward" (Morrison, 1977: 224), his father's two halves "placed cut side down, skin side up, in the coffin" (Morrison, 1977: 224); this is how Morrison sums up the brutal disdain that the class of owners and their institutions have shown to blacks. However, Guitar reserves his deepest horror for his mother's demonstration of complicity. When the millowner offers the widow the cheap compensation of forty dollars to "tide [her] over" (Morrison, 1977: 25), she takes his money and uses some of it to buy each of her children a peppermint stick on the day of the funeral. Revolted by the candy, in which he sees his mother's cowed gratitude for the white man's beneficence and her desire to use the commodity as a means to appease her children's pain, Guitar cannot bring himself to eat his peppermint. Instead,

> he held it in his hand until it stuck there. All day he held it. At the graveside, at the funeral supper, all the sleepless night. The others made fun of what they believed was his miserliness, but he could not eat it or throw it away, until finally, in the outhouse, he let it fall into the earth's stinking hole.
>
> (Morrison, 1977: 227)

Morrison understands full well the widow's dilemma. Should she not allow herself to be bought off? In a highly exploitative labor system where the notion of life insurance for black millhands is a joke, forty dollars is at least something. Should she not attempt to ease her children's experience of loss by the only means that commodity capitalism makes accessible to all? Guitar's disapproval of his mother allows the reader to grasp that her complicity is also her survival. In *Song of Solomon*, sugar as a commodity payoff is shown to be the universal substitute for satisfaction in a situation in which Guitar realizes there can be no recompense. The themes of complicity, the desire for gratification and unmediated communication, refer us back to Dufty's allegory of the young diabetic and his mother. Guitar's refusal to accept the commodity as appeasement and payoff leaves the reader with the unfulfilled desire for social relationships where neither domination nor the commodity would prevail. Morrison problematizes all the meanings present in Dufty's allegory without capitulating to moral quandary.

Toni Morrison's understanding and criticism of the widow's complicity creates another perspective for looking at R. J. Davis' statement. He is not just saying that by the mid-eighteenth century sugar had become significant in the diet of the lowest social classes. Rather, he precisely states that "the poorest farm labourer's wife" had become a regular consumer of sugared tea. There is much evidence to support the fact that male heads of households eat better than their wives and children. This was true in Britain during the coming into being and development of the industrial workforce and it is currently true throughout the Third World and most probably true in the First World as well. Mintz cites a plethora of historical documents testifying to the fact that during much of the nineteenth century British working-class children could expect bread and jam for two meals out of three (Mintz, 1985: 27). Indeed, "wives and children were systematically undernourished because of a culturally conventionalized stress upon adequate food for the 'breadwinner'" (Mintz, 1985: 130).

The same cultural logic that subordinates women to male nutritional needs also equates them with sweetness and would have all little girls believe they are made of "sugar and spice, and everything nice." Fed on tea and jam twice a day, a little girl would quite literally be made of sugar and spice. What the nursery rhyme expresses in cryptic form is, in fact, the economics of women's entry into the industrial workforce and the social consequences of this. Women who worked outside the home for pay in the nineteenth century were no more capable of putting two to three extra hours a day into preparing nutritional meals for their families than women today who hold down jobs and also raise children. If women's work in the nineteenth century brought more money into the home, the increase enabled families to consume more efficient, high energy foods that were at the same time more costly and nutritionally impoverished. In the nineteenth century this meant bread and jam, tea and sugar. Today we have Frosted Flakes, Pop-Tarts, Hostess Twinkies, Dunkin Donuts, Fruit Loops; the list goes on and on, testifying to an infinite array of equally impoverished quick-energy non-foods. These appear to buy the working housewife time, but do not achieve even that if we allow for the time spent on frequent runs to the supermarket: the shopping, the driving, clipping and sorting those nasty little coupons that merchandisers seem to give only on junk foods and lemon-scented dish detergent.

The moment at which economic integers of lesser importance come to be counted for the first time as consumers is extremely significant. The "poorest farm labourer's wife" may be anonymous, but her entry into the ranks of consumers marks a world historical event. Historically, women and children have been of secondary consequence to the creation of profit based on surplus labor. This was, of course, beginning to change in the nineteenth and early part of the twentieth centuries as many industrial jobs were broken down into even smaller units. In one of the key books on capitalist economics, *Labor and*

Monopoly Capital, Harry Braverman details how the division of labor combined with the process of deskilling to open jobs to women and children, while closing down jobs previously defined for more highly skilled and highly paid male employees. We are witnessing the continuation of the same economic process today, except that instead of the fabrication of pinheads that Braverman describes, we have banks and fast-food establishments whose employment ranks are filled by women and 15-year-olds. In the eighteenth century the "poorest farm labourer's wife" would not have counted as a producer. While she might have supplemented her husband's efforts in the field during times of increased labor demands, her primary economic function would have been reproductive: to maintain her husband's productivity and to bear and raise his future replacements. She was only slightly more significant to the ledgers that tabulate profit-making, than women and children in slavery. As long as the slave trade continued to supply a fresh source of male muscle, slave women, and particularly children, were economically expendable. Indeed, the economic significance of a female slave child was in some instances registered only by her death. One such incident opens the slave narrative of Boyrereau Brinch (Prentiss, 1810), who was brought to Jamaica in the late eighteenth century to turn his labor and whatever might remain of his life into sugar. As Brinch tells it, a host of newly arrived slaves had been set to work picking oakum, something to occupy their time and teach them the reality of organized labor before being sent out into the cane fields. Suddenly, for no apparent reason the overseer calls out a young girl slave, rebukes her in front of all the others and begins to beat her mercilessly with his whip. Finally, her belly torn, intestines extruded, the young girl agonizingly dies in the dirt. As the slave narratives make clear, beatings and murders were performed publicly for specific pedagogical purposes. As with all the atrocities committed during slavery, this one demonstrates the life and death authority of the master class. But its specific lesson has to do with the expendability of women. Young enough not to be a strong field laborer and not yet of reproductive age, the young girl had no economic purpose except that supplied by the pedagogy of her death. She was more valuable dead than alive. By comparison, the "poorest farm labourer's wife" is economically more valuable alive than dead. The relative humanity of capitalism's treatment of its economic marginals in the core areas is to redeem them as consumers.

The moment at which children and the wives of farm laborers became regular consumers of sugar truly defines the inception of the mass-commodity market. The economic importance of these, the people on the lowermost rungs of capitalism's wage and profit ladder, is to function as consumers. To have hungers that can be met cheaply and efficiently, but not substantially; to have desires that can be appeased by substitution: these render the consumer more valuable alive than dead.

CRACK: LIVING IN DRUG CULTURE

Even if we do not buy or consume drugs, we all live drug culture in our daily lives. Newspapers give us a daily dose of front-page drug-related news. Church sermons compete with public-school pedagogy in disseminating the horrors of drugs and the virtues of living drug-free. For children in public schools from coast to coast and as young as those in kindergarten, the first anti-drug lesson involves drawing an anti-drug poster. Most children draw dragged-out, brain-fried images of drug users, usually toting a smoking gun. Over this they superpose the slashed-circle logo, which, ever since the movie *Ghostbusters*, has functioned in popular discourse as the semiotic lexicon for "Don't." This is how young children of the middle classes learn to conceptualize the drug consumer as "other." By comparison, public-school anti-drug lessons in areas of high drug use are very different. Many are conducted by police officers and do not presuppose a distance between the child and drug use as does the poster exercise. Rather, children are often taught to act out a refusal when a peer pretends to solicit a drug sale. For the middle classes, anti-drug pedagogy does not call peers into question. It is, instead, structured on an opposition between "them" (the user population) and "us" (the happy, healthy, normal population). Often children's posters show smiling, well-kept people, mostly in nuclear groups, as the positive alternative to the frowning, brain-fried or dead users. The same young children who learn to separate themselves from the plight of the fantasmagoric drug-using "others" are apt to come home from school one day to report, "I survived AIDS." This is what one kindergarten-age child told me. His comment exemplifies the conceptual distantiation of security that the middle class constructs for itself and its children. Indeed, studies show that AIDS is becoming a disease of the poor, whose poverty-ravished immune systems offer inroads to viral attack. The middle class may well find a way to survive AIDS and it may find a way to keep itself and its children free of drugs. But it is haunted by the seductive fear that drugs might engulf the suburbs, snaring the wife and children in a $30,000 a year habit. Certainly, the middle class has shown little restraint where other forms of consumption are concerned.

The fear of drugs and the cultural definition of users as "other" brings to light the degree to which the middle class imagines itself as separate from the rest of society. It is as if the class as a whole constructed for itself a protective ideological bubble. Of course, it is all hypocritical because great numbers of the middle class are closet drug consumers. But the conceptual zoning off works in daily discursive practice. Out there are the homeless, the diseased, the unemployed, and, of course, the drug users. Inside the bubble, people live the illusion of unadulterated wholeness and autonomy. Each replicates a plastic-wrapped commodity inside its protective packaging bubble. In conceptualizing itself as separate from a social "other," who is at risk and in peril, the middle class lives the bad faith of its imaginary autonomy. Social disorder and ecological disaster are thought to occur only outside the bubble.

Inside the bubble, the middle class lives by a new code based on space, the policing of space, and the politics of space. Having supplanted an older class ideology based on self, possessions, and private property, the code of space accommodates a professional class whose members spend more time in offices than at home – and are more likely to live in condominiums than houses. The code of space can be detected in children's play: "This is my space, get out of it"; "My body is my space, don't touch it." This is the language that some children of the professional middle class now use. It betrays a fear of social relations and demonstrates control through the creation of boundaries. Any form of intimate contact risks being interpreted as encroachment or abuse. Such children have their own rooms, their own beds; they bathe and dress separately and privately. Out there, people mingle like fruits in an open-air market.

In chapter 5 I mentioned that in the doll's house we see an early form of the transformation of social relationships into spatial configurations. What I am getting at here goes much deeper and has to do with the conceptual enforcement of a class ideology whose end point is to banish all those defined as "other" into what amounts to an asocial no-man's land and to develop a means to control all those who inhabit the socially safe zone. The code of space offers awesome methods of social control. Parents of the professional middle class often oppose childrearing practices that are physically direct. Spankings are out of fashion. Rather, they practice and teach indirect forms of control.

One such parent told me that he and his wife let their two children "interact" so that they can become aware of each other's "personal space." But they (the parents) intervene and encourage separate play or activities when it appears that the children "are pushing each other's limits." Another parent described an "invisible fence" that her husband recently installed to control their dog. The fence is a wire buried in the ground that is electrically linked to a collar that the dog wears. If the dog attempts to cross the "invisible fence," it gets a strong shock. The animal learns its space without the owner having to establish a method of control requiring speech, touch, or gesture. The family and neighbors see the animal respecting its space without anyone having to recognize the existence of the spatial bubble.

If the spatial bubble is social hypocrisy, so too is the distinction that the anti-drug campaign asks us to make between good and bad commodities. This is the same distinction that William Dufty makes when he tells us to throw out all our sugar. Such a distinction is untenable when drugs are compared with the great majority of commodities offered for sale.

Shop at any supermarket in the United States and chances are that the brown paper bag you carry out with your groceries will have emblazoned on it an emphatic anti-drug slogan: "Say no!" This is the message stamped on every chain-store shopping bag from coast to coast. Like the poster exercise for school-age children, this warning is aimed largely at a non-drug-consuming population. It creates a sense of difference between those who see themselves as capable of saying no and their imaginary "other," who by contrast is felt to be weak and easily propositioned into saying yes. "Say no!" is the great white hope that this is all it will take to eliminate the social threat of drugs. Many of the people who carry their groceries home in "Say no!" bags will never be offered a drug in their entire lives. For them, the supermarket full of commodities presents itself as safe normalcy against the threat of unsafe commodities sold on the streets, not advertised, and not guaranteed by a brand name.

Commodity culture tells us to say yes to everything. To question a commodity strikes at the fundamental logic of a culture whose main tenets are: "If it's new, it's good; if it costs more, it's better; if it's sold, it's safe." Not to consume is to fail to exercise one's duties as a citizen. Grocery bags that preach "Say no!" would represent a contradiction in a society predicated on saying yes, were it not for the fact that in this case saying no is taken as a means for demarcating a class. Those who say yes fall to one side of the social barrier and are construed as

lawless, antisocial low life. Those who say no represent social acceptability. The fact that the grocery bag is full of pesticide-laden fruits
and vegetables, steroid-fed meats, synthetic non-foods such as diet
soda, empty foods such as breakfast cereal and chips, and a general
overdose of chemical preservatives – all of it hazardous in the long
term – is not in question. To all of this, we say yes. The admonition
against drugs precludes the possibility of raising questions about all
the other commodities defined as acceptable. We need not question
what we consume, or even that we consume. The supermarket has
done this for us.

There is another way we all experience the culture of drugs that is
just as obvious and little remarked as the "Say no!" shopping bags. I
am referring to the absolute, hard-core masculinity of drug culture.
Has there ever been in, any episode of *Miami Vice*, a highly placed
woman in the drug trade? By comparison with late twentieth-century
corporate capitalism, which has opened its doors to women executives,
the drug trade appears to be structured like an ancient robber baron
state. *Miami Vice* occasionally shows us a sister of one of the main men;
there are numerous mistresses; there was even Crockett's wife. But
there certainly has never been a "dragon lady" in the cultural
iconography of drugs – no female entrepreneurs or sales network
(even though there are reports of women's drug-dealing gangs in Los
Angeles). Nor has the media shown a highly placed woman in the
enforcement network. Can you imagine the czarina of drugs? For the
most part women in *Miami Vice* are the undercover agent "whores"
who solicit "buys" for the cops. These women are so tightly tethered
by their male cohorts that they may as well be working for pimps. If an
occasional policewoman is shown to have a bit of initiative and
independence, she is done away with in a climactic shoot-out, forfeit-
ing her life so the men can live and fight some more.

In chapter 5 I demonstrated how television's depiction of domestic
space and relationships opens the way for the resurgence of masculinity. The forms of male domination found in the sit-coms may be
insidious, but they are child's play compared to the unabashed and
violent sexism in the media's portrayal of social relationships in a
world defined by the drug economy. Its extralegality gives the drug
trade a context for imagining the most regressive forms of male
domination and portraying these in ways that are currently unthink-
able in any other generic universe. Even traditional strongholds of the
masculine imagination, such as the mystery, the spy thriller, or the
crime drama, cannot get away with the total reduction of women to

sexual objects. The hit movie *Colors* includes one bereaved mother of a slain gang member and one good wife (of the senior cop). All the rest of the women are proven bitches. They are in the movie to ally with the men and follow them around, to be in bed, and to be naked. They are described as "good lays" and except for the fact that men want "pussy" when they get out of jail, the women have no other reason for being in the movie.

Colors is like a science fiction planet where instead of two sexes, male and female, there are two male groups: the cops and the drug-dealing gangs. Contrary to the way we conceptualize the sexes as either antithetical or complementary, the two male tribes in *Colors* are mirror-images of each other. This is a movie about male bonding and male-defined space and activities. Homosexuality is tolerated because it is a version of maleness. So what if one of the gang members fucks a plastic rabbit? There is no difference between his inflated pet rodent and the women defined as sex objects. Similarly, there is no appreciable difference between the gangs and the police task force. Both occupy turf. Instead of pissing to mark their territories, as the man and wolf do in *Never Cry Wolf*, the cops and gangs lay down a spray of bullets. Both invade private domestic space; they take and hold hostages; they kill each other; and they kill people who are not incorporated in the gang/cops social division of labor. It comes as no surprise to the viewer when the senior cop in *Colors* rebukes his young buddy by calling him "a gangster just like them." As the only representative of the erstwhile police ethic that once made it possible to distinguish the good guys from the bad, the senior cop is shown to have no place in the cloned universe of cops and gangs. Hence, he is written out of any future *Colors* social scheme with a bullet at the movie's end. In a larger sense, the elimination of the senior cop, whose more humane, person-to-person tactics marked him as a relic from the past, is the movie's way of depicting what is happening in cities across the country, especially those defined as drug centers, where the police have now become a highly militarized force.

News coverage and press reports on the drug trade give rise to equally potent masculine fantasies. First of all, there is the Colombian cartel, as demonic and macho as anything seen in a Spielberg/Lucas box-office hit. Actually, very little hard information on the Medellin family exists in mainstream journalism. This leaves everything to the popular imagination. Nothing except OPEC rivals the drug cartel as the unknowable, foreign conspiracy of Third World robber barons bent on wrecking the economy, social values, and quality of life in the

United States. Both Arabs and Latins fill the xenophobic bill nicely: properly dark, properly macho, properly ruthless, properly inscrutable. By comparison, the old-style Mafia comes across as familiar, familial, even indigenous – its foreign connections boiled away in the great urban American "melting-pot." The Colombians are the unassimilable "other", the renegade and ruthless businessmen who show no interest in opening a branch office in a multistorey Plexiglas building in downtown Los Angeles like any other respected foreign capitalist.

What is not reported in the mainstream press and is most definitely left out of the media portrayals is that the Colombian drug cartel is economically quite ordinary. It replicates global capitalism entirely. "It is basically an ordinary business that has been criminalized": this is how Mike Davis defines it in his account of the Los Angeles drug gangs (Davis, 1988: 53). According to *Fortune* cocaine trafficking is "a well-managed multinational industry" (Kraar, 1988: 29). Like any other multinational, the cartel oversees the production, processing, distribution, and sale of a cheap, desired, and replenishable commodity. It has its elite line, cocaine, and its mass-market version, crack. The latter, as Davis defines it, is "an absolute commodity that permanently enslaves its consumers" (Davis, 1988: 54). The cartel's primary market has been the United States, but reports now show that it is developing a European market as well, an economically shrewd decision given the forthcoming consolidation of the European Economic Community, whose elimination of trade barriers will make drug trafficking more feasible. In the absence of any other viable employment opportunity, black youths who deal drugs have simply inserted "themselves into a leading circuit of international trade" (Davis, 1988: 52). The drug trade is so clearly structured on existing capitalist forms and so clearly organized around commodity sales that in areas where there is no crime syndicate already in existence to market the product or where youth gangs cannot be organized to handle the merchandise, ordinary small businessmen will satisfy the need for marketing outlets. This is what Pino Arlacchi found in his study of the drug trade in Verona, where local merchants meshed their activities, business skills, and commodity markets with the needs of the drug trade (Womman, 1988: i).

The fantasmagoric proportions that the cartel takes in the popular imagination has its roots in racism and in macho resentment and envy: resentment that a bunch of foreigners has outdone the great heads of legitimate multinational capitalism; and envy for the reported $500 billion a year drug trade – all of it untaxed and amassed with very little overhead expenses. After all, they do not have to pay benefits to their employees, or exorbitant rents for shopping-mall space, or pay for costly advertising campaigns.

The machismo that fuels the demonic imagination has a basis in the political economy of the drug trade and the sort of social relationships that have developed in economically depressed inner cities. In his book on the economic demography of Los Angeles, Edward Soja traces the movement of jobs and capital out of the black blue-collar areas of the city and the large-scale opening of new industries offering entry-level professional positions to white suburbanites (Soja, 1988). The selective racism and class bias of postmodern economics is obscured by the regional migration of industry. When industry is stationary it becomes the site for class struggle. When industry is mobile, it can abandon the social relations that define a particular area and opt for more favorable ones in another area. In Los Angeles, the wholesale flight of industry out of the black districts has left a wholly under- and unemployed black male population. Black women have fared somewhat better than men as many have been hired in information-processing jobs. While Los Angeles is in the vanguard of postmodern economics, other, more traditional, cities such as New York and Washington, DC, have equally high black male unemployment and equally bleak black employment opportunities. This is the labor pool tapped by the drug trade and at the heart of the macho cultural presence it projects.

In contrast to the roving macho bands of cops and gangs, the inner city as a lived space is depicted in the media as female and victimized. The pleas that go out for help, which the newspapers headline and emphasize as representative of black life, come exclusively from women, invariably single mothers. The inner city, with its dense, decaying projects, is woman defined. Depicted as unable to care for themselves, the women and their spaces are besieged and give way to the male gangs and police task forces. As the culture of drugs has it, black women are in the position of asking that their rights be abrogated for the sake of protection. In relation to the social tensions and resentments generated by feminist demands in the larger society for greater female autonomy and initiative, the drug trade offers the mainstream press an opportunity to portray inner city black women as thoroughly isolated, bereft of supportive female relationships, crying out to men for help, and being victimized by both the gangs and the cops. One could not ask for a better scenario for retrenched racism and machismo. Black women are seldom interviewed and never quoted in groups, daily-life networks are never shown, instead black women are depicted raising children single-handedly (and badly), isolated in their apartments, in their journeys to work, in their jobs. The only voices recorded are the pleas for help; the only testimonies accepted are those that show women as ancillary to or dependent on men.

Such reportage offers the white middle class yet another way to conceptualize itself as different from its social "other." White professional women can pat themselves on the back each time they read about the plight of black women in the inner city, knowing that they are not dependent on men for gifts or protection. It is not threatening to the white middle class to know that black women are coping against insurmountable odds; after all, this is what they have done ever since slavery. The erasure of urban black women's networks and cultural life provides an ideological support for the conceptualization of feminism as a profession whose jurisdiction goes no further than the office, the university, and the suburb.

CRACK: THE PAYOFF

The advent of crack as a mass-market commodity for the urban underclass has occasioned a range of police enforcement tactics and court actions the like of which have not been seen in this country and are rivaled only in Britain, where anti-immigration sentiment and mobilization against the IRA have produced a similar enforcement and surveillance agenda against a racially defined underclass. The war on drugs commands a big budget, three-quarters of which goes on enforcement, while the scant leftovers get divided up for treatment and education programs (Dillin, 1989: 8). Enforcement is primarily aimed at the street dealers, with massive sweeps that net a thousand or more low-level, replaceable salesmen. The war on drugs defines the city as a war zone, and its residents, if not the enemy then some special class of non-citizens who do not have the rights assumed by those recognized as citizens. What is most astounding, indeed terrifying, is the lack of uproar against current enforcement tactics on the part of any social group except the beleaguered complaints of the American Civil Liberties Union. The all but blatant acceptance of surveillance, curfew, arrest sweeps, identity checks, and illegal searches demonstrates the degree to which people in the inner cities have been defined as "other," even by the black middle class (Davis, 1988: 44). The mainstream population need not see trends in juridical and police actions as posing a threat to their lives because, after all, members of the professional middle class do not have to make their domestic space regularly available for searches; they do not risk eviction when their sons or daughters are arrested on a drug charge; they are not threatened with prosecution for having failed in their parental responsibilities when their children are under indictment. These are some of the measures being proposed, in some cases enacted, and, in a few instances, being tested in the courts. The only difficulty is imagining the middle class in the position of its social "other."

Mass culture sometimes apprehends social relations in such a profound way as to depict these in all but transparent figurations. Everything that I have been saying about the conceptualization of the drug-using population as "other" is articulated in the movie *Alien Nation*. This is an amazing cultural metaphor. In it the user population is cast as aliens from outer space, whose history includes just enough cultural indices to allow the audience to associate the aliens with black Americans. The aliens, called "newcomers" in the movie, are a society of shipwrecked humanoids, biologically engineered to be slaves. They are highly adaptable and can perform all the menial and dirty tasks that the earth population shuns. They live in "slagtown," the newcomer ghetto, and are generally peaceful until they get hold of the "drug." It is suggested that the newcomers stink and that the males have much larger penises than males from earth. Finally, like the emancipated slaves who were arbitrarily named by Freedman's Bureau officials, the aliens were similarly named by their quarantine officers. The movie's alien protagonist is, thus, Sam Francisco.

The most interesting consequence of the social division between users and non-users is its effect on race relations in the earth population. Once the user population has been completely separated and conceived as alien, the non-user population, which in the movie is the Los Angeles Police Department, is free to develop multiracial and multiethnic relationships. There are blacks and Chicanos as well as Anglos in the social mainstream of the police force – all joined together in the brotherhood of non-users. What is more, the non-users can see themselves as perpetually different from the slagtown "others," forever safe, because the movie's highly addictive super-drug has no effect on earthers, whereas aliens on the drug lose all thought of social life. They think only of obtaining more and more of the drug. And if they ever overdose, they transform into murderous superbrutes.

Alien Nation is not without its liberal solution. Aliens can forsake the drug; and, like Sam Francisco, who makes friends with a white cop, they can look to integrating with mainstream society. Male bonding is the movie's method for bridging social "otherness." Buddies work together, trade jokes, and get drunk: the earther on alcohol, the alien on sour milk. Drinking establishes social cohesion; drugs separate people from monsters.

Prior to the marketing of crack, critics whose aim was to establish a relationship between drugs and capitalism generally sought to reveal the intimate connections between the drug trade and the foreign policies of western nations. The most informative and hair-raising study along these lines is *The Great Heroin Coup* by Henrik Kruger, which supplies information on enough drug-financed covert intelligence operations to keep several TV drug dramas going for a number of years. These operations include destabilization campaigns, arms deals, the infiltration and subversion of radical movements, training camps for death-squad torturers, and political assassination: all of them paid for out of the heroin trade and performed by gangsters simultaneously on intelligence agency payrolls. What Kruger does not set out to prove but nevertheless implies is that the fortunes of left-wing struggles in Latin America have been connected with the control of the underclass in the United States by their curious relationship to the drug trade and to those who run the trade. This is a contemporary version of the eighteenth-century relationship between slaves in the New World and the laboring class in Britain, whose fortunes were interconnected and controlled by the sugar trade. The consumption of the underclass in the First World, which ensures its dependency and impoverishment, also provides a means for exercising control over the underclass in the Third World (whether that underclass comprises eighteenth-century slaves or twentieth-century guerrilla fighters).

Where the global trail of "dirty tricks" financed by heroin establishes a connection between drugs and the foreign policies of capitalist states, crack demonstrates the intimate connection between drugs and commodity capitalism. If a commodity is illegal, is it also outside capitalist economics? One of the residual tendencies inherited from the counter-cultural movement of the sixties is to assume that if a particular object or practice is aberrant – or abhorrent – to mainstream culture, it is also aberrant to the system as a whole. This may have been the case with homegrown marijuana and campus chemistry lab LSD, but it is definitely not the case with crack. No other commodity marketed today better exemplifies Marx's formula for capitalist economics than crack. "Money begets money" (Tucker, 1978: 335) is how Marx put it when he defined economic exchange as M–C–M (money–commodity–money). The capitalist buys a particular commodity for no purpose other than to sell it at a higher price. The commodity is "nothing but exchange value" (Tucker, 1978: 328). Crack as a commodity could not be better engineered for profit-making, with its cheap, replaceable labor, minimal costs of processing, and a mass market in sales. At \$25.00 a hit, sometimes less, crack is truly a mass-market commodity. If in 1750, the poorest farm labourer's wife could afford tea and sugar, by the late 1980s women, children, and the unemployed can be regular drug consumers.

Crack also has important consequences for the definition of use value. Marx conceived of economic circulation based on use value by the formula C–M–C (commodity–money–commodity). If I produce a product, such as embroidered blue jeans – or, in a less artisanal mode, if I produce use value in the knowledge I make available to students – then according to the use value formula, I trade these for money or a salary and with it I buy all the other commodities necessary for daily life that I myself do not produce. What crack means for the street dealer is the capitalization of use value. For the street dealer, crack is devoid of use value. It is only a means of getting money, which is itself a means of getting the real objects of desire, the commodities that are truly felt to have use value: the clothes, jewelry, cars, sound systems, and weapons that are named by every street dealer in every interview as the whole point of dealing drugs.

It is not completely true that crack is "nothing but exchange value" or a means of obtaining commodities. Use value exists in what the consumer sees in the commodity (Tucker, 1978: 328). However, the capitalization of use value extends to the buyer as well as the seller of crack. No matter how intensely desired, no matter how satisfying the "high," crack produces the absolute atomization of the individual. Rather than enabling or articulating social relationships, it eliminates the social and puts the individual in relation to the fetish commodity. The economics of addiction is the negation of the social. Its repercussions are manifest in the growing number of crack-addicted mothers who abandon their children to the care of friends and relatives, and the great number of crack-addicted teenagers who see their parents only as candidates for theft. The morality of child abandonment and theft need not be the only issue. What is at stake is the moment when a person's relationship to others matters less than his or her relationship to a commodity, and when it is felt that a commodity has the power to gratify in ways that relationships to people cannot.

In 1945 Theodor Adorno wrote *Minima Moralia*, a collection of observations on daily life that are as pertinent today as in the aftermath of the Second World War. The whole of the book is written against "The withering away of experience" (Adorno, 1974: 40). The loss of dimensions, the narrowing of focus that condition our personal relationships replicates our relation to objects. As Adorno puts it, objects have become purely functional, narrowly defined by their specific use. The commodity object is wholly contained in its purpose. It has no other larger use or meaning, no "surplus," nothing that escapes inscription in its commodified functionality. As a drug, crack induces the ultimate "high"; as a commodity, it absorbs the "high" in a serial desire for the next one. Crack is wholly functional. Its pleasure is the duration of the commodity. It is wholly consumed in the moment. There are no leftovers except for the tiny brightly colored caps that come with its packaging. This is not a fistful of "pot" sold in a Baggie off the supermarket shelf. In its packaging alone, crack can be seen as a mass-market commodity. Think of it: hundreds of thousands of tiny plastic-capped vials supplied by one system of production and filled by another. Young children look for the plastic caps in urban playgrounds, on the street, at the beach. They collect them and trade them with their friends, turning crack caps into commodity meanings in the same way that children in the fifties collected and traded bottle caps from Nehi and Coke.

8

EARTHQUAKE KITS
The politics of the trivial

Because ours is a commodified culture, we do not have access to social relationships and historical processes except by way of the commodity form. This does not mean, as some would argue, that history no longer exists; that because we cannot get in touch with the referent, we live in history's simulated afterglow. Nor does it mean that the social has been wholly negated, leaving us to savor the hollow pleasures of alienated relationships and fetishized desires. Rather, the contending social forces that shape history come together for us in daily life. Varied, but wholly routinized, random, but programmed, daily life appears to be of little consequence, so close that we live it as if by second nature. Nevertheless, if we are to grasp history, we must begin to recognize its presence in the mundane. Dismissed as trivial, fragmented, and fetishized by its assimilation to the commodity form, daily life is our site of convergence with the historical. Thinking critically about daily life can provide a means of grasping contradiction. Such insight gives impetus to the transformation of capitalist culture.

The challenge is to apprehend daily life dialectically and in so doing have access to contradictory social meanings. This is a method that Theodor Adorno put into practice in his collection of essays *Minima Moralia*. Adorno clearly saw the trivial as a site of historical convergence, whose most potentially transformative instances crop up in children's play. Observing a child playing with a toy truck laden with barrels, Adorno observes that play replicates production under capitalism. But it is an allegory. "The little trucks travel nowhere and the tiny barrels on them are empty" (Adorno, 1974: 228). Play is "purposeless." It mimics production, but is not productive because it generates only pleasure. The point Adorno is making is that purpose is the phenomenological dimension of exchange value. In its purposelessness, child's play is the creation of use values. If we truly grasp what Adorno is saying, then we must hold in our consciousness the powerful and impossible recognition that this instance of play both wholly affirms and negates capitalism. Such recognition cannot be contained or managed, but is, instead, impelled to quicken the utopian imagination. Adorno's allegory is a means of questioning, not play, but work itself. How might productive activity be gratifying? Is it possible to conceive of labor in ways not bent to purpose?

Not all instances of daily life hold forth utopian possibilities. In most, the replication of capitalist social formations is so completely naturalized by the function of ideology that we fail to grasp them as allegories. None, however, are so wholly fetishized as to be seamlessly fused with capitalism. After all, the commodity form, which by definition is the negation of the social relations of production, nevertheless requires the social for its production. This is the contradiction of the commodity form; and it is on the basis of this contradiction that we can begin to prise open the objects and practices of daily life. The following observations seek to reveal the historical dimensions of what must be one of the most degraded and trivialized objects of daily life: a school earthquake kit.

THE EARTHQUAKE KIT: A POSTMODERN FALLOUT SHELTER

Remember these are our children, *YOUR* children, and those precious, faithful, loving, smiling faces whom we all cherish more than anything else in the world are our responsibility, *NOT* the school district's, *NOT* the city's but *OURS AS PARENTS.*

(Letter from Condit Elementary School to all parents, Claremont, California, November 1989)

Many public and private schools (including pre-schools) in suburban areas of California are currently asking that parents provide each of their children with an earthquake kit. The promotional materials sent home with children or through the mail focus on fear for the children's safety, and define parents as negligent if they fail to supply the recommended kit. Fliers sent out by parent–teacher organizations often couch the request for kits in terms that promote feelings of parental guilt. The burden of guilt is especially aimed at mothers who work outside their homes. One such school flier that I received features the tearful face of a child whose grief-stricken plea is given in quotation marks: "Daddy is in LA, working, and I can't get Mommy on the phone. Who is going to take care of me?" Such representations of family demonstrate how anti-feminist backlash is translated into the most common throwaways of daily life. The flier accepts father's work in LA as normal. After all, this is the suburbs. But it questions why mother is not at home and throws the child's distress in her face. The implied subtext is that the safety of the child depends on mommy's being there and that she assume full responsibility for childrearing.

The late eighties gave rise to a number of anti-feminist backlash phenomena, including the withdrawal of federal support for abortion and a tremendous upsurge of anti-abortion sentiment that lent itself to sensationalization in the media. This was also the time when the press played up the "mommy track" as a way of demonstrating to professional women the futility of their efforts to gain job equality with men. At a more mundane level, the condemnation of women's increasing entry into the workforce found its way into countless public-interest columns featuring women who would rather be at home baking bread for their families than out killing themselves 9:00 to 5:00. The most notorious and widely publicized of the media back-lash phenomena was the McMartin Preschool case, involving the alleged sexual abuse of children in day care by their teachers, which ran for five years, cost the taxpayers of California $13,000,000, and gave the press unlimited opportunity to dramatize parental fears over day care. Many working mothers asked to comment on the McMartin case, expressed uncertainty and guilt over their own need for day care and their choice of going out to work. Many confessed that the only way they could imagine allaying their fears was to quit work and stay at home with their children. Broadly felt anti-feminist backlash puts the working mother in a position where she must either acquiesce to societal pressure and function more like a mother, or suffer the burden of guilt for her decision to work. With respect to the McMartin Preschool case, the interview procedures employed by the press singled women out, put them on the spot as if to accuse each and every mother of negligence for the simple fact of having a child in day care. They created a situation in which any response a woman might give was already framed by accusation and bound to generate feelings of uncertainty and guilt. The result was the inability to use the McMartin case as a means of examining the whole question of private day care. The five years during which the courts and the press kept the

McMartin case alive did not give rise to the radical notion that day care need not be private, but might be communally organized and controlled. Nor did any woman interviewed ever suggest that what we really need is free universal day care, even though almost every mother who works recognizes that a major portion of her salary is spent on day care and after-school care. In isolating the day-care consumer, making mothers and fathers feel that they have to negotiate day care alone, as individuals, and in making women experience guilt about working, the dominant forces of society prevent radical social critique and the possibility of imagining daily-life alternatives. The situation is no different in the case of the earthquake kit. The fliers portray natural disaster as "imminent," promote fear with drawings of seismic waves and 8.8 readings on the Richter scale, and finalize their message by pointing the finger of guilt at mothers who are not at home when disaster strikes. Questions that would uncover the social meanings of the kits are not asked – not even imagined.

What is an earthquake kit? I grew up in California, but had never had one, nor heard talk of such a thing. After fifteen years spent in other states, I came back to find that the hallucinogenic stories of earthquake that conditioned my childhood had been replaced by grim survivalist strategies. Rather than images of a quake-liberated California severed from the rest of the country and floating out to sea like Ernest Callenbach's Ecotopian island, people were now circulating rumors of impending doom. I found myself wondering just what went into an earthquake kit. Crash helmets and bandages sprang immediately to mind. After all, what can one do in an earthquake? Certainly, there are no magical devices that might lift a child out of the quake zone or protection to encase his or her body until the earth and rubble settle. So what, indeed, is a parent supposed to put in an earthquake kit? Canned fruit, juice, Beefaroni, a plastic spoon, and a few moist towelettes: these are some of the magical commodities for survival. Individually boxed and labeled, every child in every classroom is to have a kit.

For its generalized triviality, the earthquake kit exemplifies one of the most important features of the commodity form: it promotes the notion of democratized consumption. Its ability to do so is a dramatic demonstration of what Marx meant by commodity fetishism. As he defined it, the commodity form is the negation of the labor and social forces of production. "In it the social character of men's labor appears to them as an objective character stamped upon the product of that labor; because the relation of the producers to the sum total of their own labour is presented to them as a social relation, existing not between themselves, but between the products of their labour" (Tucker, 1978: 320). In commodity capitalism, we have no way to experience or conceptualize relationships between people except as these are defined by the exchange of commodities. As they exist and circulate, commodities come to be the form by which we know the social. Ranked uniformly on shelves, openly available, ever replenished and abundant, the display of commodities is the alienated and fetishized embodiment of the desire for social democracy – and, therefore, its cancellation.

The power of commodity fetishism is truly great. It produces and maintains the notion of social democracy on the basis of consumption even while economic life in this country is stretched between the growing numbers of the fabulously wealthy and the more rapidly growing numbers of families in substandard housing, on poor diets, bereft of medical care, or altogether homeless. Such vast economic disparity is made to appear asymptomatic with respect to the commonly accepted norm of social democracy embodied in the ever-present two-storey, air-conditioned shopping malls and the ubiquitous sprawl of suburban strips. The latter features all of life's necessities: fast food, video rentals, discount drugs, haircuts, frozen yoghurt, pet hospitals, dry cleaning, and nail care. The ideology of commodity capitalism is that we all trade equally in the culture.

The notion of democratized consumption, broadly expressed in the media and built into the architecture of the suburbs, finds its most mundane expression in the earthquake kit. There is no elite line of kit for the Beverly Hills crowd, nor do the wealthy get bigger kits. Every kit is very like every other kit. Shaped by the view of survival in a society where, it is implied, the cataclysmic destruction will have a levelling effect on more than just the built environment, the commodity form achieves a universality that it does not fully have in the real world of economic exchange, where actual commodities represent elite and mass-produced lines. Indeed, I would argue that the standardization of the earthquake kit, which is not a product of corporate decision but is instead produced by the myriad individual parents who assemble the kits, includes the utopian notion of a fully classless society where we might indeed all trade equally in commodities. The levelling of social difference is integral to the way we tend to imagine disaster in late twentieth-century capitalism. It was the basis of a form of gratification that the "disaster movies" of the late seventies rendered experiential. What makes the child's school earthquake kit a succinct metaphor of commodity capitalism is its absolute equation of survival with the commodity form and its prefiguration of a new society universally defined by commodity communality. The latter is a fully contradictory notion, as there can be no communality defined on the basis of the commodity form. This, however, does not negate the articulation of utopian desires even while these are contained and negated.

I make a point of the utopian possibilities present in the earthquake kit because such features are rarely present in the commodities that define our daily lives. Although mass produced, most commodities are marketed for specific consumers and often include stylistic details that designate class, race, and gender differences. Such differences may appear to be wholly stylistic and superficial, but they have their roots in a society in which difference means social inequality. Because the stylistic features of commodities are so taken for granted they serve to normalize and perpetuate notions of inequality and subordination. To show how this is true I would like to compare the earthquake kit with an analogous, equally trivial object, used every day by millions of schoolchildren: the lunch-box. Where the earthquake kit suggests the levelling of social difference, school lunch-boxes marketed today display the absolute substantiation of gender polarity. Some lunch-boxes are done up in bold primary colors: red, yellow, and blue; and are decorated with militaristic robot or mutant action figures, most of them male, driving super-powered vehicles, and shooting state-of-the-art weapons. These are for boys. In contrast, some lunch-boxes are done up in soft blue, turquoise, and pink, the colors that designate the girls' section in every department store, and have as their motifs images of Barbie, My Little Pony, Care Bears, and a plethora of hearts, flowers, and rainbows. There are a few crossover lunch-boxes: those depicting Tweety Pie or Bugs Bunny. But children learn to see these as dated with respect to the mass-media toy market that generates a new cast of cartoon commodities every year. Besides, the choice of Bugs Bunny represents gender ambiguity in a culture where commodity consumption so clearly valorizes compulsory gendering.

Color is as much a sign of gender – and in this case, gender dominance – as is the subject-matter of lunch-box design motifs. The same bright primary colors are replicated in the Fisher-Price logo and toy line and in the Mcdonald's "McKids" logo and clothing marketed through Sears. To be masculine is to be associated with the dominant corporations of the childhood commodities market. In contrast, the colors that the mass market associates with being female have no corporate referent, except Baskin-Robbins 31 Flavors ice-cream. But, as everyone knows, sugar is for little girls.

If, in the earthquake kit, standardization and universality suggest a classless, raceless, and genderless society, these potentially egalitarian social characteristics are contained by another feature of the kit that fully cancels its utopian possibilities. This is the absolute individuation of the kit. One kit per child. No sharing, trading, or pooling of goods either between siblings or on a classroom basis. Only individuals will be saved to emerge from the Cataclysm as discrete social integers, whose autonomy has been affirmed by their unmediated relationship to their commodities.

The earthquake kit defines a starkly different social vision from that suggested by its historical antecedent: the fallout shelter. In many respects, the earthquake kit replicates the suburban fallout shelter, compressed, as it were, into compact dimensions for its atomized consumer/survivor. The fallout shelter was already particularized, but on the somewhat larger scale of the nuclear family unit. Political cartoons of the Cold War era made much of the exclusionary nature of fallout shelters. Families had to decide whether or not they would let their neighbors into their private shelters. Consensus held for the sacred right of private property, while limited space and food supplies were the commonly circulated rationales for a notion of survival and the perpetuation of society based on the family as the prime unit of consumption. Indeed, fallout shelters resembled mini-supermarkets in their neatly stacked shelves and abundance of canned goods.

The earthquake kit replaces private property with the portable, expendable commodity. This would be another potentially democratizing aspect were it not for the fact that real property ownership in this country is concentrated in fewer and fewer hands. This is particularly the case as family farms shut down, as interest rates rise, and as land and construction prices make the American dream of home ownership an impossibility for many Americans. This was not the case in the fifties, when an upwardly mobile and growing middle class laid claim to the suburbs and dramatically proclaimed its right to property ownership in a landscape devoted to designating the boundaries of possession. The backyard neatly fenced or walled, the driveway marked off with a hedgerow, the foundation girdled with shrubs, the neighbor's property-line etched by the swathe of a lawnmower, nature was reinvented to embody the map and deed to property. The middle class tested the territorial limits of property by digging swimming pools and fallout shelters, thus laying claim to deep space. And it set the upper limit of its property with ever taller TV antennas. By comparison, the middle class of the nineties includes many deterritorialized members. While there are still houses in the suburbs, many middle-class families and singles now live in gated communities, townhouses, and condominiums. Rather than claiming its right to private property in the traditional form of land and home, the class aggressively demonstrates its right to an uninterrupted flow of commodities and leisure activities. The earthquake kit represents the transformation of private property into the postmodern notion of space, and space into the commodity form.

CAMPING OUT AT GROUND ZERO

In addition to the supermarket, the fallout shelter is also a distorted reinvention of family camping. Many people stocked their shelters with the same medical kits and camping gear that they originally bought for use in tent or trailer. Indeed, as the fear of nuclear holocaust began to subside, families hosted slumber parties in their otherwise unused shelters. Children played house in them. Like the barbecue, backyard camping is a typical suburban family activity. By pitching a tent and cooking out in the backyard, families renegotiate the terms of their space and create new meanings out of their landscaped property rights. Backyard camping puts the wilderness back into the denatured accoutrements of landscape, especially at night when darkness blurs boundaries and the neighbor's dog is apt to sound like a wolf. Built into the backyard and approximating family camping, the fallout shelter generates meanings much larger than its intended Cold War purpose. This is not the case with the earthquake kit, whose complete condensation to the commodity form allows the expression of only the most residual traces of past meanings. The kit fully eliminates the dimension of practice from camping and replaces this with a recommended tube of sunscreen and a "solar blanket." The latter is a high-tech camping commodity, developed out of space research and demonstrating that whatever family camping might have meant in the past, it is today fully commodified and fully assimilated to the defense industry. For most of us, camping conjures up notions of practices inherited from Native American culture. The ideology and iconography of Indians is so much a part of camping lore that we tend not to recognize what is really the most important influence on camping: the military. Many of us first experienced camping as a Boy Scout or Girl Scout, but few of us recognized the history of colonialism, army field manuevers, and military equipment as the defining principles of camping. My own memories of scouting include learning how to read trail-blazing signs, tie knots, pitch a tent, and how to cut your best friend's arm or leg to let snake venom out. With such naturalized memories, I was taken aback when a friend announced that he was going with his son's Cub Scout troop for their weekend camp-out on a docked battleship. Such a trip affirms the implied military content of all camping experiences. The fact that as a Girl Scout I never camped out on a battleship has practically nothing to do with gender. During the Cold War, and particularly the Suez Crisis, battleships and their use were wholly integrated with the notion of defense. With missile technology and obsolescence, the battleship has become accessible for a cultural use, which is in every respect ancillary to its military function, as a field for camping.

Besides the more general connection between camping and the military, there is a fundamental link between camping and the culture of nuclear war. This relationship goes much deeper than the backyard fallout shelter, which is finally only one of its manifestations. A friend, Alexander Wilson, has conducted extensive research on the landscapes of late twentieth-century capitalism (Wilson, 1991). His observations document how nature has become an element of design, whose use in industrial or leisure installations functions to naturalize the built environment. Wilson's research details the integral relationship between the development of recreational land use and the nuclear industry. The model is the Tennessee Valley Authority (TVA), where a once natural topography of rivers, lakes, mountains, gorges, and valleys has been reworked into an immense, interlocking grid for the production of hydro and nuclear energy, weapons production, nuclear research, and waste storage. All of this is, then, interlaced with campgrounds, hiking trails, and boating and fishing facilities. The natural setting provides a context in which the production of nuclear energy is felt to be at one with the natural processes of the environment. Similarly, the wholesome notions we attach to family camping lend a sense of safety to the nuclear industry. We might scoff at the idea of camping at Three Mile Island, but millions of Americans will camp in the TVA industrial complex and swim at a seashore whose recreational purpose is secondary to its function as a cooling system for a nearby nuclear plant.

I mention the TVA not to bemoan the passing of nature, or to deplore the fact that we cannot just walk off into uncharted tracks, there to experience at first hand a more balanced ecosystem. The point is that nature for us has been replaced by the "out of doors," a wholly commodified realm necessitating an array of specialized equipment and vehicles for its use and enjoyment. Whatever activities people once performed in nature to ensure survival and cultural vitality have been transformed into their commodified simulacrum: recreation. In the United States, the development of recreational family camping with tent or trailer and Coleman stove in the fifties, and the now more prevalent RV with gas-powered fridge, heating, air-conditioning, and TV, is based on the maximum individualized consumption of transport, camping equipment, and campsites. Such sites may not all be part and parcel with the nuclear industry, but most "natural" lands are contiguous with military installations, power plants, or industrial sites that service the nuclear industry. The privatized family campsite nestling on federal or state land is not separate and antithetical to the defense industry. Rather, family recreational land use, like the trees, rocks, and waterways of the once natural world, function as alibis for the transformation of ecological topographies into nuclear systems. In developing the notion of simulation, Jean Baudrillard has commented that for us natural topographies no longer have a reality separate from their mapped simulations. As he puts it, the map is ours before we encounter the land. In fact, it produces our apprehension of the land ("c'est elle qui engendre le territoire": Baudrillard, 1981: 10). The transformation of nature into simulation is best exemplified by the "self-guided hiking trail." These come equipped with brochure and map whose numbered reference-points indicate pieces of vegetation and geological phenomena, also numbered in correspondence with the map. Just as the path is posted with warnings – "Stay on Trail" – so too does the map function to reduce our experience of canyon, woods, or meadow to its designated reality. Nature is an alibi for our appreciation of space as program. Children run up the path accumulating numbers. For them, the "self-guided trail" is a Nintendo-type video game. The numbered plants and rocks are no different from the video bleeps they learn to negotiate as they maneuver a Nintendo hero through a wilderness of programmed obstacles and events.

The backyard fallout shelter is not the dystopian antithesis of some more wholesome experience of family camping. Rather, it lifts the individuated, nucleated, and commodified recreational experience out of public lands and plants it in the backyard. However, because camping is a social practice and as such includes numbers of people, activities, and situations, it also includes the potential for alternative enactments. The Women's Encampment at Greenham Common in Britain represents an important cultural form, whose radical potential was recognized and reproduced by women at the Seneca Lake Peace Encampment and by men and women at countless other less publicized sites, such as the nuclear plant at California's Diablo Canyon. Such encampments made use of the practice of camping in order to reveal and critique the militarization, nuclearization, and male domination inherent in camping as a form – and in the larger society. Such radical reversal is no longer possible when social practices are compressed into the shorthand of the commodity form itself. The earthquake kit eliminates the activity of camping from the form and with it the possibility of redefining social relationships. The Greenham Encampment represents a form of guerrilla theater that cannot be realized on the basis of the commodity form. If we open up an earthquake kit, we reveal no more than the commodities that comprise it. The juice, soup, and chapstick – these embody the simulated remembrance of how they might have been used if purchased for a camping trip, but they do not give access to social practice or its guerrilla theater reversal.

A SACK OF POTATOES AND A STREET LINED WITH HOUSES

The translation of the fifties' fallout shelter into the earthquake kit of the nineties is facilitated by the way in which commodity fetishism erases historical referentiality, making nuclear war generated by superpower rivalry equal to natural disaster brought about by tectonic plate movement. However, the fear of nuclear war in the fifties was never a wholly political experience. Rather, it was apprehended as a new form of natural disaster whose fearsome mushroom cloud was every bit as much a cultural icon as MGM's "twister" that carried Dorothy off to Oz. The mushroom cloud represented the sum total of Cold War paranoia gathered up into its billowing mass. Children born during the post-war Baby Boom were the first generation to grow up with TV and the media diffusion of miniature mushroom cloudlets into suburban living-rooms. Many Baby Boomers who are parents today have in their socialization the experience of powerlessness in the face of a disaster that was equated with the natural and therefore perceived as beyond control. Disempowerment gave birth to hope for salvation in a hole in the ground. "The bomb" might be dropped any day at any one of the likely epicenters from which the children of the fifties plotted the distance of their school, their home, their likelihood of survival. Children today do not have such fantasies, a fact brought home to me while viewing with my children a video of Jerry Lee Lewis' career: *Great Balls of Fire*. "What's that?" asked my 7-year-old, who could not understand why Lewis' adolescent girl-friend shrieked, cried, and hid her eyes from her own TV screen. There it was, the mushroom cloud on her TV set, its image sending the terrified girl into a fit of pathetic sobbing. Our children may not recognize the mushroom cloud but this does not mean that their socialization is free of paranoia. Rather, the disempowerment that characterizes late capitalist culture generates the sort of free-floating fear that Don DeLillo articulates in his novel *White Noise*. Here "toxic events" are a daily reality, brought home to the suburbs by the same corporations that produce life's sustaining commodities and then provide the technology for cleaning up the toxic by-products of commodity production.

The Berlin Wall has been dismantled, its bits transported and sold as souvenirs in the "free" world. But the fears that fueled Cold War paranoia have not been dispelled. Rather, they hover about as an unspecified postmodern condition whose persistence is manifest in the return of the fallout shelter – reinvented as parody in the earthquake kit. The reinvention of cultural forms is related to the repetition of historical forms which the culture embodies and articulates. To grasp the presence of history in parody, we have only to recall the place where history, parody, and the experience of class disempowerment all come together: Marx's *The 18th Brumaire of Louis Bonaparte*. Marx's intent is to demonstrate how the revolutionary forces of 1848 were contained and defeated. His analysis turns on the recognition that historical forms tend to repeat themselves at moments when history does not achieve revolutionary transformation, but instead disintegrates into the counter-revolutionary perpetuation of dominant class interests. Following Hegel's notion that the important events and personages of history occur "as it were, twice" (Marx, 1984: 15), Marx suggests that they produce themselves first as tragedy and the second time around as farce. Indeed, one of the aims of *The 18th Brumaire* is to render a caricature of Louis Bonaparte as the grotesque parody of his uncle. The more profound aim is to demonstrate how parody is produced out of the manipulation and containment of what might otherwise have been revolutionary class interests.

In *The 18th Brumaire*, Marx documents the complex political maneuvers and conflicting class relationships that brought about the counter-revolutionary cancellation of 1848. These may not have all been readily available to the various classes and class factions engaged in shaping the historical moment, but all may well have grasped their cultural embodiment in the parodic figure of Louis Bonaparte. In culture, we live historical processes, even though we may not apprehend such processes fully – or even historically. In culture, history is represented to us. Cultural analysis can be a means of apprehending the historical forces that might otherwise not be immediately accessible. Just as Marx recognized parody in the manner by which Louis Bonaparte quashed the Paris proletariat of 1848, so too do we discern a parody of fallout shelters and Cold War paranoia in the earthquake kit. The reasons why this is so transcend the trivial characteristics of the kits themselves and have, instead, to do with the complicated relationships of class to history, and historical forms to capitalism.

In assessing the political situation of the revolutionary urban proletariat, Marx finds that a number of factors contributed to the defeat of their aspirations for radical historical change. These include a rivalry between the landed and merchant factions of the bourgeoisie that Louis Bonaparte was able to play to advantage, and the stifling of socialist tendencies amongst the petty bourgeoisie. However, Marx suggests that what finally cancelled the possibility of broad social revolution was the failure of the peasantry to come to revolutionary consciousness and ally with the urban proletariat. Indeed, Marx maintains that the class interests of the peasantry resided in such an alliance, but these could not be realized because of the particular historical and economic constraints on the peasantry at the time of the revolutionary uprising. Marx looks back to the revolution of 1789 and affirms that the peasantry had indeed undergone dramatic transformation "from semi-villeins into freeholders (Marx, 1984: 126)." The Napoleonic Code certified and regulated their right to and use of small-holdings. However, by 1848 Marx sees the small-holding as fundamental to the containment of the peasantry as a potentially revolutionary force. In his words, "the small-holding peasants form a vast mass, the members of which live in similar conditions but without entering into manifold relations with one another. Their mode of production isolates them from one another instead of bringing them into mutual intercourse" (Marx, 1984: 123). Indeed, "each individual peasant family is almost self-sufficient; it itself directly produces the major part of its consumption and thus acquires its means of life more through exchange with nature than in intercourse with society" (Marx, 1984: 123). This is how Marx elaborates the economic basis of the failure of the peasantry to come to consciousness as a class. Wholly isolated, wholly fragmented into individuated production units, the peasantry had no material basis for class cohesion, no productive practices that might have linked members across family lines and geographic regions. In Marx's view, the countryside was composed of:

> A small-holding, a peasant and his family; alongside them another small-holding, another peasant and another family. A few score of these make up a village, and a few score of villages make up a Department. In this way, the great mass of the French nation is formed by simple addition of homologous magnitudes, much as potatoes in a sack form a sack of potatoes.
>
> (Marx, 1984: 124)

If the final image is derogatory, it is meant to dispel romantic notions of peasant communality. In the United States, some sixty years ago, William Faulkner demonstrated that the notion of small-town cohesiveness and solidarity amongst sharecroppers is a view that obtains only from outside the system. For those inside *The Hamlet*, the economic scarcity that promoted rivalry between its residents generated a population of swindlers, fast traders, and unfeeling dealers. For the sharecropper, as for the mid-nineteenth-century French peasant, fragmentation produced disempowerment. Marx describes a broad mass of people whose circumstances ought to have provided impetus for revolutionary action, but whose mode of production prevented the social or conscious realization of communality.

Marx goes on to argue that the peasantry, unable to represent itself politically, found representation in the parodic form of Louis Bonaparte, who aped the style and mouthed the policies of the peasants' liberator: Napoleon. This is the politics of disempowerment and thwarted class consciousness. Like a "sack of potatoes," the peasantry was incapable of expressing or enforcing its interest as a class and therefore sought representation in an authority figure, who, as Marx maintained, had demonstrated his power to subordinate competing social forces to executive decree and who might, then, protect them from other social classes. In this way, Marx saw the disempowered peasantry as the most influential factor of the counter-revolutionary process. The break-up of the feudal system into small-holdings was lived as a liberatory moment in the Napoleonic period, but was negated some forty years later when the small-holding laid the foundation for the crippling fragmentation of the class. The transformation from liberation to containment gives rise to parody as the cancellation of class affirmation.

Just over a decade ago Marx's observations on the French peasantry were brought to bear on an important debate between Marxist scholars over whether or not late twentieth-century capitalism has created the conditions for the emergence of a new social class. Taking a landmark position, Barbara and John Ehrenreich maintained that we are indeed witnessing the formation of a new class, which they designated the professional/managerial class, or PMC (Walker, 1979: 5–45). The Ehrenreichs claimed class status for the PMC on the basis of a recognizable political history that in the past has ranged from liberal reformism to the radicalism of the New Left, and on the basis of the PMC's tension-fraught relationship to capital, which includes a measure of autonomy even while the class as a whole is dependent on capital for jobs and salary. The Ehrenreichs' position was contested by Stanley Aronowitz, who argued that technical workers and managers do not constitute a class, but rather represent a number of social strata with divided loyalties (Walker, 1979: 213–42). Central to Aronowitz's refutation of the Ehrenreichs is a distinction Marx makes between a class that recognizes itself as such and acts to affirm its interests, and a class like the French peasantry of the mid-nineteenth century that relinquishes its interests to a superior authority. The peculiar way in which the PMC appears to be a class but does not affirm itself as such offers a way of understanding the relationship between disempowerment and parody that we find in the earthquake kit. This is how Marx put it:

> In so far as millions of families live under economic conditions of existence that separate their mode of life, their interests and their culture from those of the other classes, and put them in hostile opposition to the latter, they form a class. In so far as there is merely a local interconnection among these small-holding peasants, and the identity of their interests begets no community, no national bond and no political organization among them, they do not form a class.
>
> (Marx, 1984: 124)

Clearly, the PMC is composed of millions of families whose economic conditions separate their mode of life, their interest and values, and their trend-setting culture from those of the other classes. One might even argue that the PMC stands in hostile opposition to the other classes, although such polarized class interests are, as Aronowitz points out, a little blurred at the upper reaches of the class, whose senior managers are seldom at odds with corporate heads, and at the bottommost reaches, whose nurses, teachers, and social workers often find themselves in alliance with more oppressed groups. However, the aspect that most clearly underscores the failure of the PMC to attain class status is the same lack of cohesion that Marx attributed to the French peasantry. Marx's description of the French countryside has found a parallel in the middle-class suburb, where "there is merely a local interconnection among family units and the identity of their interests begets no community." While we might broadly point to the way in which the politics of Reagan and Bush have served the interests of many members of the PMC, the class as a whole has no political or social institution for the expression of class interests. Apart from parent meetings at the neighborhood elementary school or church groups in areas where religion is strong, middle-class families rarely see each other except to say hello as they leave for work or drive their children to school. The suburb and the gated townhouse "community" are the ultimate expressions of a purely "local inter-connection" among families. The class that promotes itself on the basis of competition between its members and rivalry across class factions disintegrates upon the absolute individuation of its members. Such rivalry is put aside only where matters of security are concerned. Many suburban areas now sport signs declaring the area "Protected by Neighborhood Watch." This means that residents watch out for "suspicious" individuals on their streets, and agree to call the police if they notice a neighbor's house being robbed. Rather than represent-ing community solidarity, neighborhood watch is a proclamation of the sacred nature of private property. Residents remain fully autonomous while preserving each other's property and boundaries.

The lack of a viable middle-class community has become especially evident in Los Angeles as the city nightly sprays malathion over the property and gathering protests of its residents. For over five years, the State of California has conducted an all-out pesticide campaign against the Mediterranean fruit fly, which to date has been found only in suburban backyards, but is, nevertheless, felt to pose a tremendous threat to the state's multi-million-dollar fruit industry. Despite the wholesale helicopter spraying of the state, township by township, forty droplets of pesticide per square foot, the fly continues to thrive. The consumer is sprayed for the sake of distant corporate growers.

The middle-class puts plastic bags over its roof vents, covers its cars, brings its pets in, and makes use of town councils to voice protests. But the courts turn a deaf ear. The class that in the fifties vaunted its property rights with backyard fence, TV antenna, and swimming pool, now finds the security of its domain wholly negated by the Vietnamization of public air space. Individual property rights are swept aside in order to preserve the powerful agricultural interests that dominate state politics.

Where Marx saw the French peasants of 1848 fragmented into individual production units, each in intimate relation to the soil and disconnected the one from the other by the lack of socialized production methods, I would similarly describe the professional middle class as fragmented with respect to its mode of social reproduction. In doing so, I do not want to deny the significance of people's relationships to the means of production. The fragmentation of daily life has its basis in the high division of labor that characterizes the professions. Social life does not precede the economic organization of capitalism. Rather, it is integral to it. However, for many of us the immediate experience of capitalism as a structure occurs in our daily lives, and it is here that we can begin to make connection with the economic features of capitalism. The basic social unit of the PMC is the family, whether this be a single-parent household, a two-income family, or a more traditional male-headed nuclear family. Each family unit exists for the purpose of recycling exchange value. Where the peasant family as a productive unit was in direct exchange with nature, the PMC family, as a non-productive unit (Walker, 1979: 12), functions to define an autonomous circuit of consumption based on private home, private car, and the individual use of the local shopping mall. The PMC family does not require "intercourse with society" for its survival. A PMC family unit sits alongside another PMC family unit. Several score of these comprise a residential tract, each with its own shopping mall and gas station. Several score of these make up a suburb, perhaps a town. The simple addition of homologous units produces the pattern of the houses along a street but this does not constitute the basis for community.

To the extent that the middle-class suburb is defined in terms of consumption, the transformation of daily life might begin with the development of socialized consumption. However, as consumption is currently defined, each family unit, and more often each family member, functions as an individual consumer. The weekly allowance sets children free to meet their needs and desires independently.

Convenience foods allow family members to feed themselves separately and at any hour of the day. The duplication of home leisure technology and the diffusion of audio and video shops turn families into assemblages of atomized consumers of leisure. The extreme individuation of consumption coupled with the feeling that gratification is something that only individuals can experience (and this localized in a specific brain or body site) makes it extremely difficult for anyone in the middle class to imagine what socialized consumption might be and what sort of pleasures it might produce. Almost everything we do in daily life, we do as individuals. In fact, we are told that to do otherwise would be inefficient. So each one of us makes a separate trip to the dry cleaners, a separate trip to the supermarket, a separate trip to the video rental. The atomization of consumption precludes the development of social relations between consumers even while it maximizes profits and the overall recycling of exchange values. When socialized forms of consumption do come into being, these are generally disparaged or seen as aberrant. For instance, car-pooling is acceptable for mothers who have to get their children to and from school and baseball practice, but it is not seen as a mode of transport that any truly successful men would use. As the movie *Mr Mom* makes clear, only men in low-level managerial positions and on the brink of being laid-off would ever stoop to sharing rides. Success is the affirmation of the individual as a maximizer of consumption. Similarly, cooperative food-buying is something that only unreconstructed hippies would enter into. A network of families who organize buying in bulk from wholesale distributors and share the responsibility of breaking down the food into smaller units and distributing it is thus viewed as backward and wasteful of time and energy. In fact, such a mode of consumption allows people to buy wholesome food cheaply, to organize their efforts into concentrated expenditures of labor and time, and to enter into reciprocal communal relationships. I make a point of socialized consumption, particularly the formation of cooperatives, because such practices reverse the influence of capitalism on daily life. They also offer a radical alternative to the impoverished possibilities currently being held out to us by mainstream currents in popular culture criticism. The consensus is that individuals "make do" (Fiske, 1989: 25) or "cope" (Fiske, 1989: 30), but are not in a position to transform commodity culture. As consumers, we make meanings out of the commodities produced by capitalism. Sometimes we make resistant meanings, but all meanings are assimilated by capitalism for the production of fresh commodities. As

John Fiske puts it, we resist bourgeois cultural values by ripping our jeans, but Calvin Klein sells them back to us and makes a profit on our resistance. By comparison, socialized consumption is not resistant but alternative. It is not capable of being assimilated back into capitalism.

I mention socialized forms of consumption because the individuation of consumption is fundamentally disempowering for most people, even many of those in the PMC with big pay-checks. The curious effect of consumer society is its distortion of our social reality. We live the inverted notion that to be independent is to negotiate daily life on our own. The more tasks we accomplish as individuals, and the more commodities we have to show for it, the more in control of our lives we are. The ideology of consumer society defines atomization as strength, while bonding with others to facilitate social reproduction is a sure sign of weakness and insufficiency. In his book on consumer society, *All Consuming Images*, Stuart Ewen considers the relationship between the ideology of consumption and its political enunciation: democracy. His aim is to demonstrate how the expansion of the mass market enhanced the popularly held belief that class has to do with status and is wholly defined by one's ability to consume. As Ewen sees it, "By the middle of the nineteenth century, the expanding market in appearances was helping to feed a notion of class defined primarily in *consumptive* rather than productive terms, highlighting individual, above common identity (Ewen, 1988: 62; author's emphasis). He goes on to show how the ideology of consumption has come to be equated with democracy. The availability of mass-produced commodities made it possible for the expanding middle class to buy the accoutrements of class formerly associated with the elite. Democracy became a style rather than a political practice. The middle class only had to represent success. The difficulty Ewen faces is how to resurrect a notion of class based on an individual's relationship to production given the awesome, spell-binding, and overwhelming influence of the ideology of consumption. Indeed, as Ewen devotes his book to tracking the power of the commodity form across the centuries and throughout different forms of cultural production, from advertising to architecture, there is very little room to demonstrate how people might come to grasp their relationship to production and recognize this as somehow determining. As Ewen points out, such a revelation would be particularly problematical for those in the middle class – presumably the majority of the book's readers – whose experience of self and social reality has been so assimilated to the ideology of consumption. Nevertheless, Ewen argues in line with the Ehrenreichs and Aronowitz that:

> The stylish ephemera of the new "middle class" existence was more of a symbolic fringe benefit, a *cultural wage*, which permitted its recipients to identify with the interests of the upper classes, while occupying a relationship to power that was more akin to that of the working classes. In its symbolic identification with power, this "middle class" performed, and continues to perform, a political function; it effects divisions among people who otherwise might identify with one another.
>
> (Ewen, 1988: 64; author's emphasis)

I would extend Ewen's argument in line with the discussion on the PMC and in relation to Marx's analysis of class in *The 18th Brumaire* to say that thinking of class in terms of consumption, however ideological, has fully to do with the lived experience of the middle class, for whom lack of control in professional life (and the defeat of the air-traffic controllers is a good example), and the failure to come to grips with such lack of control, represents itself in falsely construed notions of control over the social reproduction of daily life. This includes consumption, but many more activities and phenomena as well, such as the definition of domestic life, the family, and the family's preservation and security. The impression that consumption has come to replace one's relationship to the means of production in the determination of class actually upholds the dominance of production. In failing to apprehend itself as disempowered and bought off, the middle class relinquishes itself to the interests of the uppermost echelons of the corporate state – those who own the means of production, set corporate and national policy, and make the decisions that ultimately determine social life.

The disempowerment of the middle class reveals itself not only in the divisive rivalry that it promotes between individual members and, as Ewen points out, across class factions that ought to "identify with one another," but most poignantly in its fears for the future. Incapable of enacting, let alone conceptualizing, class interests, the middle class strives for the preservation of its individual members. In the absence of a class-defined sense of future, which can be grasped only when a class lives historically, individual members project future out of the lives of their offspring. The daily politics of the middle class is the effort of all of its individual members to ensure the security of its children on an individual basis. Each must be protected from drugs,

disease, random gang violence, and finally earthquakes. The point of
these observations is not to evoke pity for the beleaguered middle
class, whose members clutter their lives with possessions, eat for
entertainment, and drive Saabs to the office, passing on their way
numbers of unemployed youths bearing signs: "Hungry, will work for
food." Rather, the aim is to recognize how privilege masks disempowerment and how disempowerment serves the interests of
capital and class domination.

Extending her economic and politcal analysis of the PMC, Barbara
Ehrenreich has written a book documenting the social psychology of
the middle class, whose apt title, *Fear of Falling*, captures the experience of class disempowerment that I have been describing here.
Ehrenreich maintains that one of the reasons why the middle class
qualifies as a class in the political sense, is that throughout its history
it has so actively generated fantasy fears for its continuation.
Ehrenreich maintains that such fears bespeak the recognition of being
in competition with other social groups; hence, a sense of class.
However, because the class is not communally defined, its notion of
future can be generated only out of images of procreation and the
family. The interest of the class is to make sure its offspring do well in
school, attain professional careers, marry within the class, and
achieve higher incomes than their parents. The focus on the family as
the site at which class interests are defined means that any threats
generated outside the family in politics and history cannot be directly
apprehended by the professional middle class, but rather find
metaphoric translation into familial terms. Thus Ehrenreich reminds
us that the Cold War paranoia of the fifties found familial translation
into fears over juvenile delinquency. Powerless in the international
sector, the class saw itself as unable to ensure its own reproduction
from one generation to the next. Its offspring might become "de-
viant," fail "to adjust to the larger (middle class) scheme of things"
(Ehrenreich, 1989: 23), and slide into a lower-class lifestyle complete
with duck-tailed haircut and black leather jacket. Similarly, in the
sixties, the middle class translated its compliance with a national
politics of global aggression into self-doubt over its wayward youth.
Middle-class parents lived the counter-cultural youth movement as
retribution for "permissive" childrearing practices (Ehrenreich,
1989: 68–74). The juvenile delinquent of the fifties; the counter-
cultural youth of the sixties; and today, the innocents of the nineties,
who at any moment might be struck down by random gang violence,
fall victim to drugs, or disappear in the rubble of a schoolyard – these

are the hysteric fantasies of a class whose only sense of future is its next generation.

FAMILY PHOTOS

Finally, parents are asked to put a snapshot of the family in the earthquake kits they assemble for their children. Have we so thoroughly become an image culture that all remembrance is reduced to the photograph? The family, tossed in amongst the canned commodities, is the expression of fetishized relationships and reified memories. But the photograph has not only to do with the assimilation of social relations to the commodity form. The request for a family snapshot bespeaks the parent's needs and fears, not the child's. Promoted as a reassurance for the child, the family snapshot actually documents the class fear that the family might be at risk. Failure to conceptualize the family and document its existence, no matter how fetishized, would be to recognize that the class has no politics but its image.

AFTERWORD

Some thirty years ago the great Argentine writer of the fantastic, Julio Cortázar, wrote a story that today offers a telling point of comparison with a particular daily-life occurrence that most of us take for granted: the commuter traffic jam. The story, "Autopista del Sur," depicts homeward-bound motorists caught in progressively slowing traffic until they eventually find themselves in a bumper-to-bumper stoppage. Cortázar's use of the fantastic is to take the trivial and turn it into the means of wholly redefining reality and experience. Many of us have been stuck in a freeway gridlock. The impossibility of movement where there is supposed to be uninterrupted flow makes this a frustrating and claustrophobic experience. As in Cortázar's story, the reason for the traffic jam, a wreck or road repair work, is seldom visible. There is only the endlessly compacted, four-lane-wide mass of cars and drivers overheating themselves. The time of entrapment always seems longer than it is. Five minutes feels like half an hour. The fantastic dimension of Cortázar's story is born out of his use of temporality, which he heightens and distorts to an even greater extent than we normally do when stuck in traffic. The motorists seem to be trapped for days – perhaps months. Their entrapment becomes the basis of the radical transformation of the absolute fragmentation and atomization ordinarily associated with a freeway journey, where millions of car-cocooned individuals jockey for position, each wholly isolated from the other. With no convenient off-ramp in sight and not even the slightest indication of an eventual resumption of flow, Cortázar's motorists transform the freeway into a community. Neighborhood groups three cars up and three cars back come into being. Systems of barter are developed between motorists with supplies of food and water, and these are later extended to include feral peasant bands who inhabit the margins of the freeway. People's relationships with each other have nothing to do with who they were in the world beyond the freeway, where they lived or worked, how much they earned. Rather, all social relationships are newly defined on the basis of mutual needs and communal reciprocity.

The end of Cortázar's tale is the resumption of movement. This sunders the freeway communities. Relationships stretch until they disintegrate as cars and motorists speed up, fall back, change lanes and once again become atomized commuter units. Like many utopian thinkers, Cortázar finds ways to imagine community born out of the breakdown of capitalist social structures. In contrast, corporate capitalism invents new ways to check the desire for community and sell it back to us in the form of a commodity. Many of today's motorists trapped in a freeway gridlock need never question their atomization, let alone establish communication with the similarly trapped commuter in the adjacent automobile. Who needs community when you can "reach out and touch someone" with a car phone? What is more, there are special rush-hour radio programs with giveaways for car-phone trivia quiz respondants and a hotline for car-phone music requests. "I'm on the San Bernardino, barely moving; play me some Eric Clapton." There are even isometric exercises promoted in books, magazines, and on TV that make it possible to turn your car's dashboard, steering wheel, seat, and roof into a mini gym. The commodity ploys designed to promote the gratifications of alienation are the abundant and accessible means of countering dissatisfaction and stifling the desire to imagine alternative practices and social formations.

In the first chapter I challenged the reader to recognize instances of contradiction in daily life and to search out utopian possibilities in social practice. The strong but facile temptation is to assume that the mere discovery of utopia in mass culture somehow constitutes the transformation of daily life. Such is the basis of a simplistic and celebratory notion of cultural politics. The real struggle is to use the recognition of utopia as impetus for fundamental social change.

REFERENCES

Adorno, Theodor (1973) *Negative Dialectics*, London: Routledge and Kegan Paul.
——(1974) *Minima Moralia*, London: Verso.
——(1982) *Prisms*, Cambridge MIT Press.
Alexander, Sally (1976) "Women's work in nineteenth century London: a study of the years 1820–50," in Juliet Mitchell and Ann Oakley (eds) *The Rights and Wrongs of Women*, Harmondsworth: Penguin.
Barrett, Michele (1980) *Women's Oppression Today: Problems in Marxist Feminist Analysis*, London: Verso.
Baudrillard, Jean (1970) *La Societé de Consommation*, Paris: Denoel.
——(1975) *The Mirror of Production*, St Louis: Telos Press.
——(1981) *Simulacres et Simulations*, Paris: Editions Galilee.
——(1988) *Selected Writings*, Stanford: Stanford University Press.
Benjamin, Walter (1969) *Illuminations*, New York: Schocken.
——(1986) *Moscow Diary*, Cambridge: Harvard University Press.
——(1989) *The Dialectic of Seeing: Walter Benjamin and the Arcades Project*, Cambridge: MIT Press.
Birman, James (1979) "Disneyland and the Los Angelization of the arts," in Myron Matlaw (ed.) *American Popular Entertainment*, Westport: Greenwood Press.
Boston Women's Health Book Collective (1976) *Our Bodies, Ourselves*, New York: Simon and Schuster.
Bowlby, Rachel (1985) *Just Looking*, London: Methuen.
Brown, Wilmette (1983) *Black Women and the Peace Movement*, London: International Women's Day Convention.
Carby, Hazel (1986) "Sometimes it jus' bes' dat way," *Radical America* 20: 9–22.
Davis, Mike (1988) "Los Angeles: civil liberties between the hammer and the rock," *New Left Review* 170: 37–60.
Deerr, N. (1950) *The History of Sugar*, vol. 2, London: Chapman and Hall.
Dillin, John (1989) "US wrestles with drug strategy," *Christian Science Monitor*, July 3.
Dufty, William (1976) *Sugar Blues*, New York: Warner.
Ehrenreich, Barbara (1989) *Fear of Falling*, New York: Pantheon.

REFERENCES

Ewen, Stuart (1988) *All Consuming Images*, New York: Basic Books.

Ewen, Stuart, and Ewen, Elizabeth (1982) *Channels of Desire*, New York: McGraw-Hill.

Fiske, John (1987) "Miami vice, Miami pleasure," *Cultural Studies* I: 113–19.

——(1989) *Understanding Popular Culture*, Boston: Unwin Hyman.

Fonda, Jane (1984) *Women Coming of Age*, New York: Simon and Schuster.

Franco, Jean (1986) "The incorporation of women: a comparison of North American and Mexican popular narrative," in Tania Modleski (ed.) *Studies in Entertainment*, Bloomington: Indiana University Press.

Frith, Simon (1981) *Sound Effects*, New York: Pantheon.

Glubok, Shirley (1984) *Doll's Houses: Life in Miniature*, New York: Harper and Row.

Gould, Stephen J. (1982) *The Panda's Thumb*, New York: W. W. Norton.

Hall, Stuart (1986) "On postmodernism and articulation," *Journal of Communication Inquiry* 10: 5–60.

Hatch, James V. (ed.) and Shine, Ted (consultant) (1984) *Black Theater USA*, New York: Macmillan.

Haug, Wolfgang (1986) *Critique of Commodity Aesthetics*, Minneapolis: University of Minnesota Press.

Hebdige, Dick (1979) *Subculture: The Meaning of Style*, London: Routledge, Chapman and Hall.

——(1987) *Cut 'n' Mix*, London: Routledge, Chapman and Hall.

Hooks, Bell (1988) "Overcoming white supremacy," *Zeta* 1: 24–7.

Horkheimer, Max, and Adorno, Theodor (1972) *Dialectic of Englightenment*, New York: Seabury Press.

Huggins, Nathan Irvin (1971) *Harlem Renaissance*, New York: Oxford University Press.

Hutchins, Grace (1987) "The double burden," in Charlotte Nekola and Paula Rabinowitz (eds) *Writing Red: An Anthology of American Writers, 1930–1940*, New York: Feminist Press.

Illich, Ivan (1982) *Gender*, New York: Pantheon.

Inman, Mary (1987) "The pivot of the system," Charlotte Nekola and Paula Rabinowitz (eds) *Writing Red: An Anthology of American Writers, 1930–1940*, New York: Feminist Press.

James, C. L. R. (1963) *Black Jacobins*, New York: Random House.

James, Selma (1975) *Sex, Race, and Class*, London: Falling Wall Press.

Jameson, Fredric (1979) "Reification and utopia in mass culture," *Social Text* I: 135–48.

Kraar, Louis (1988) "The drug trade," *Fortune* 20: 29.

Lott, Eric, (1988) "Blackface and blackness: politics of early minstrelsy," American Studies Association Convertion, Miami.

Lukács, Georg (1962) *The Historical Novel*, Boston: Beacon Press.

——(1971) *History and Class Consciousness*, Cambridge: MIT Press.

Marx, Karl, (1984) *The 18th Brumaire of Louis Bonaparte*, New York: International Publishers.

Mechling, Elizabeth Walker, and Mechling, Jay (1983) "Sweet talk: the moral rhetoric against sugar," *Central States Speech Journal* 34: 19–32.

Mercer, Kobena (1987) "Black hair/style politics," *New Formations* 3: 33–54.

Mintz, Sidney (1985) *Sweetness and Power*, New York: Viking.

Modleski, Tania (1982) *Loving with a Vengeance*, New York: Methuen.

Morrison, Toni (1970) *The Bluest Eye*, New York: Washington Square Press.

——(1977) *Song of Solomon*, New York: New American Library.

Ohmann, Richard (1988) "History and literary history: the case of mass culture," *Poetics Today* 9: 357–75.

Prentiss, Benjamin F. (1810) *The Blind African Slave or Memoirs of Boyrereau Brinch*, St Albans, Vt: Harry Whitney.

Radway, Jane (1984) *Reading the Romance*, Chapel Hill: University of North Carolina Press.

Schlesinger, Stephen, and Kinzer, Stephen (1983) *Bitter Fruit*, New York: Doubleday.

Soja, Edward (1988) *Postmodern Geographies*, London: Verso.

Spivak, Gayatri (1987) *In Other Worlds*, London: Methuen.

Tompkins, Jane (1985) *Sensational Designs: The Cultural Work of American Fiction 1790–1860*, Oxford: Oxford University Press.

Tucker, Robert C. (ed.) (1978) *The Marx–Engels Reader*, New York: W. W. Norton.

Walker, Pat (ed.) (1979) *Between Labor and Capital*, Boston: South End Press.

Williams, Eric (1964) *Capitalism and Slavery*, London: David and Charles.

Willis, Susan (1987a) "Fantasia: Walt Disney's Los Angeles suite," *Diacritics* 17: 83–96.

Willis, Susan (1987b) *Specifying: Black Women Writing the American Experience*, Madison: University of Wisconsin Press.

Wilson, Alexander (1991) *The Culture of Nature: Popular Landscapes from Disney to Chernobyl*, Toronto: Between the Lines Press.

Women's Studies Group, Centre for Contemporary Cultural Studies, University of Birmingham (1978) *Women Take Issue*, London: Hutchinson.

Womman, Karen (1989) "Europe's cocaine boom confounds antidrug war," *Christian Science Monitor*, June 10.

Wynter, Sylvia (1979) "Sambos and minstrels," *Social Text* 1: 149–56.

INDEX